D1374683

THE NATIONAL YOUTH THEATRE

Zigger-Zagger, Jeannetta Cochrane Theatre, 1967.
Zigger (Tony May) leads the fans at the City End.

SIMON MASTERS

THE NATIONAL YOUTH THEATRE

LONGMANS YOUNG BOOKS

LONGMANS YOUNG BOOKS LTD

LONDON AND HARLOW

Associated companies, branches and representatives throughout the world

SBN: 582 16340 4

ACKNOWLEDGEMENTS

The publishers gratefully acknowledge permission to use the following illustrations in this book: Graham Attwood (3b, 6, 13, 19, 62a, 62b, 70, 72, 81, 83); BBC TV (61); *Daily Mail* (7, 27, 79, 82); Fox Photos (17); Douglas Glass (12); John Haynes (frontispiece, 14, 22, 25, 32, 33, 35, 36, 38, 40, 51, 53, 64, 66, 67, 75, 85); John Hopkins (59); Alexander Low (facing 1, 21); John Minshall (71); Eric Moore (15); Photo-Reportage (58); Photopic (Paris) (47, 48); David Sim (5, 43, 78); Crispian Woodgate (74).

Designed by Bernard Crossland

PRINTED IN GREAT BRITAIN BY
LOWE & BRYDONE (PRINTERS) LIMITED LONDON

Foreword

This book is an introduction to the National Youth Theatre which thousands of young people every year apply to join. It is a straightforward book which tells the story of the National Youth Theatre in a straightforward way but with a liveliness which is typical of the National Youth Theatre itself.

This foreword is an introduction to the book and there is absolutely no reason to waste a second reading it, except for one thing. The book is written by a member of the National Youth Theatre. It is an excellent account of the work of the National Youth Theatre, its aims and its struggles, its successes and misfortunes. Perhaps because the author has been so closely involved in these he does not dwell upon what seems to me to be the greatest merit of this unique company. Reading it one would not imagine that the National Youth Theatre had high artistic aims, and dealt with drama and with poetry in a very subtle form. Yet in this way the book is a true reflection of the work and outlook of the National Youth Theatre for it does not encourage its members to indulge in 'arty' talk and fanciful theory. It prefers to practice, not to preach. It gives young people a genuine artistic experience without making any song and dance about it, and this seems to me the real beauty of its work.

Ralph Richardson

President of the National Youth Theatre.

Contents

List of illustrations

'It seems to be one of the few completely classless institutions that England has produced.'

A GERMAN CRITIC

'For its members the Youth Theatre provides the most collective dramatic experience since the American Group Theatre—while the public gets a fresh, clear, bold, colourful production.'

BERNARD LEVIN

Michael Croft talks to Martin Jarvis
about Henry V. *Sadlers Wells, 1962.*

1 The history and aims of the National Youth Theatre

It is fitting and perhaps ironical that the school founded by that great Shakespearian actor, Edward Alleyn, and bearing his name, should prove, some three hundred years later, to be the springboard for one of the most significant theatrical and educational events of the last 50 years—the foundation of the National Youth Theatre.

In 1955 Michael Croft was an English teacher at Alleyns. His first novel, *Spare the Rod*, was published that year, and at the same time, after completely re-organising the school's dramatic society, Croft was coming to the climax of a series of remarkable Shakespearian productions. These, involving almost the whole school in some department of production, were of such a standard that *The Times* theatre critic wrote of one of them: 'Considered as a school play it was a miracle.' With the instantaneous success of *Spare the Rod* Croft decided to give up teaching and devote his time to writing. Consequently Alleyns lost a unique English teacher, and the pupils lost their extremely popular play director.

They felt this loss so keenly that in 1956 a group of boys approached Croft with the request that he should continue to produce plays with them outside school. Croft agreed. Thus the Youth Theatre was born.

During the summer holidays of 1956 these boys worked with Croft on a non-existent budget, with no facilities and under appalling conditions. Simon Ward, a member of that original company, recalls: 'The tiny room with theatre posters drooping from the walls was in absolute chaos. It was packed with boys rehearsing, reading, typing, making telephone calls, poring over booking charts, studying ground plans and making costumes. The noise was indescribable and as all this energy overflowed, through the door and down the stairs, I remember expecting irate neighbours to appear at any moment, if only to see what was causing such a disturbance in such a peaceful part of

London as Dulwich. I was immediately informed that as a special, first day treat, I could begin by sticking stamps on to 1,000 envelopes. I left several hours later with an awful taste in my mouth, the noise noticeably several decibels higher than when I had arrived, and wondering just what sort of organisation I had joined.'

Chaotic?—Yes! But it was a chaos tempered by a unity of effort and zeal which won through against daunting odds. In September 1956 *Henry V* was presented at Toynbee Hall, Aldgate East, and won some notice from the critics, who found this schoolboy company a refreshing change and were impressed by the obvious fiery enthusiasm of the cast.

Dark days followed in plenty and the early history of Youth Theatre endeavours is fraught with crises and calamities. The only thing which held the company together and saved the Youth Theatre from obliteration was the loyalty, determination and irrepressible spirits of those original Alleyns' boys.

There was, for instance, the time when, still operating without any financial backing, the company took *Henry IV Part 2* to Manchester in August 1957. On arrival they found that there had been no advance publicity, no advance booking, and accommodation for the company had not been secured. Only the spontaneous loyalty and enthusiasm of the company saved the day. They paraded in full costume through the streets of Manchester towards Piccadilly bringing traffic to a total halt. In Piccadilly Gardens they enacted a whole scene in full costume to a gaping audience of passers-by and to the accompaniment of nearby workmen's pneumatic drills. It is gratifying to report the performance so captivated the workmen that they laid down tools to watch the company.

Despite adversity, however, the company expanded. Croft was already recruiting from seven London schools, and by 1958 this had grown to all schools in the Greater London area. In May 1958 the Youth Theatre received its first, direct financial aid—an annual £500 grant from the King George's Jubilee Trust.

In 1959 the company was drawn from all the southern counties, and in 1960 it became a national organisation, members being drawn from the whole of England, with the inclusion of girls for the first time.

For the Youth Theatre 1960 was an important year. It saw its first foreign tour—Holland—plus an appearance at the international Paris *Théâtre des Nations* Festival, officially representing Britain. Financially things improved with a Ministry of Education grant to set up permanent headquarters plus an annual grant for administration. The

2

In the early days NYT heroines were played by boys as in Shakespeare's time. In Hamlet, *1959/60, Ophelia was played by Hywel Bennett. On page 59 there is a photograph of Hywel Bennett as Hamlet in 1963.*

ERRATUM

The photograph on page 59 is of Simon Ward, not Hywel Bennett, acting Hamlet in 1963.

Richmond (Hywel Bennett and Richard (Neil Stacey) in Richard III, *Scala Theatre, 1963.*

King George's Jubilee Trust grant was trebled, and the Gulbenkian Foundation awarded a single £1,000 grant. Lastly, 1960 saw Croft's modern-dress production of *Julius Caesar*. This production was destined to be a landmark in Youth Theatre history. It became the most revived, most highly praised Youth Theatre venture until *Zigger-Zagger* seven years later.

In 1961 the Youth Theatre was registered as a charity under the title 'The National Youth Theatre'. An NYT Club was established in 1962 for all-the-year-round activities, and to enable members to keep in contact with one another between the main seasons.

The company first appeared in the West End in 1959, and returned each year so that by 1964 its summer season was almost an integral part of the West End scene. By 1964, however, Simon Ward, the last surviving member of that original Alleyns' company, had left the NYT to turn professional, and Croft was faced with a difficult decision. Either he could continue to recruit a large number of new members and put a huge raw company into the field, or he could keep newcomers to a minimum, a much safer line of approach.

With his great faith and optimism in young people Croft made a characteristic 'nothing ventured: nothing gained' decision—to accept as many new members as possible and launch the largest NYT season in the history of the company. He decided to present two plays, each with its own, separate acting company, one of which was to be *Coriolanus*—not Shakespeare's easiest play—dressed in the immediate pre-World-War-One period. In an interview with Bernard Levin, Croft described the forthcoming 1964 season as: 'The most exciting thing that the Youth Theatre has done since it began.'

This was the first time the NYT had put two companies, independent of one another, into the field. At this time the NYT had only two permanent members of staff—Michael Croft the Director, and David Fournel (who had been a member of the original Alleyns company) the Secretary. But with the help of a great number of old ex-members, such as Geoffrey Reeves, who is now directing with the Royal Shakespeare Company, the NYT was confidently able to face the immense problems such an undertaking involved. The success of that 1964 season laid the foundation for the future development of the NYT.

In 1965 the company received one of the greatest honours of its brief but spectacular career. Croft was invited by the National Theatre Board to take the NYT to the Old Vic for its summer season, something neither he nor any of the company had dared even to contemplate.

Mark Antony (David Weston) rouses the mob.
Julius Caesar, *Queens Theatre, 1960.*

The NYT in 1966 made a break, for the first time, with its tradition of presenting only Shakespeare. In April a small company presented Shaw's *The Devil's Disciple*, and in the summer, also for the first time occupying two West End theatres simultaneously, Jonson's *Bartholo-mew Fair* and David Halliwell's brilliant *Little Malcolm and His Struggle Against the Eunuchs* ran side by side with *Antony and Cleopatra*.

There was a logical progression from one year to the next, as the company, its capabilities and ambitions all increased. And so it was logical that in 1967 Croft and his staff attempted the most ambitious season ever. The NYT refuses to stand still, even more to take a

Coriolanus, *Queens Theatre, 1964, in a 1914 setting. The Tribunes
(Derek Seaton and Leslie Robarts) with Menenius (David Stockton).*

retrograde step, and when faced with a challenge the company is at
its best. Throughout its history it has proved time and time again
that the impossible can be beaten.

In 1967 the company occupied three theatres for a performing
season which lasted six weeks. Five plays were rehearsed and presented. *The Tempest* and *Henry IV Part 1* were aimed directly at
school GCE candidates. *Romeo and Juliet* ran for a week in a small
town outside London prior to a two-week European tour. This culminated in Brussels where, with the Sadlers Wells Opera Company, it
was the official contribution to British Week. *Henry V*, rehearsed in
only a week (becoming known as the 'instant-Henry'), played at
Sunderland with many young people from the north-east in the cast.

Most important of all, however, was the production of *Zigger-Zagger*
by Peter Terson. Continuing the policy begun with *Little Malcolm*—
that of presenting new, modern plays—Croft took a futher step by
commissioning Terson to write a play for the NYT. His only qualifica-
tion was that it should cater for a very large cast. The result—
Zigger-Zagger, the NYT's greatest triumph since *Julius Caesar*.

So, to look back: in its twelve years' existence the NYT has staged
thirty-eight productions. Its membership is drawn from all parts of
Britain and numbers, at the moment, about 2,000 young people. From
an inconspicuous beginning in a small Aldgate hall its annual summer

season has become a unique aspect of the theatrical scene. Its intention is to encourage young people to appreciate the arts of the theatre whether as audience or participants. It is a theatre for youth by youth, offering to its members an exceptional insight into the practical workings of theatre. As an ensemble company it offers the chance to work in a team, all members equally sharing responsibility. It is true to say that throughout its history the NYT's greatest strength has been in its members: in their loyalty and determination to succeed.

It has also set alight the Youth Theatre movement which was virtually unknown before, and in addition to the Youth Theatre groups founded by the NYT, such as the very fine Manchester Youth Theatre, it has encouraged the growth of many other provincial Youth Theatres so that there are now about 150 such groups in the country. The NYT runs an advisory service for Youth Theatre groups, and has played a part in the foundation of a great many of them. No longer is it an impoverished, inconspicuous boys' society; now it is part of a nation-wide movement for which the NYT holds the torch!

Cleopatra (Helen Mirren) in Antony and Cleopatra, *Old Vic, 1965.*

2 How to join the National Youth Theatre and how it operates

Membership of the NYT is open to all young people in Britain between the ages of fourteen and twenty-one. It is not usual for students already at Drama Schools or Universities to be accepted, although, of course, any member may remain with the company until the upper age limit regardless of whether he goes to University or Drama School. Even young people who go into full-time work can take part if they have an enlightened employer who, as in past cases, will allow his employees to take their holidays to coincide with the season. Some members have given up their jobs each summer simply so that they can take part, and in the early days of Youth Theatre when National Service was still compulsory, members of the company who had been drafted into the army were allowed to take their leave during the production period. Most members stay with the company until the upper age-limit, though this may involve them in considerable effort and sacrifice.

The intake machinery starts to operate in the early spring of each year when every secondary school in the country is notified by circular of the forthcoming auditions. It is hoped that the schools will bring the circulars to the notice of pupils who will write for auditions. Many, many more young people apply of their own accord by letter to the secretary, perhaps having seen an NYT production, noting the fact that all applications must be in before the end of February.

There is no Youth Theatre type. Michael Croft is not looking for brilliant actors. He is simply looking for responsible young people who have an interest in some aspect of theatre work, be it stage management, set building, wardrobe, lighting, tape-recording, or acting, and who are prepared to give up their school holidays in order to become part of the NYT team.

In Michael Croft's own words: 'Ideally he (or she) must be able to look after himself, willing to take on any job that's going, not get

The designer, Christopher Lawrence, at work on a set.

big-headed, and keep a sense of humour in times of stress and strain. He may never have acted in his life, maybe he can't act anyway, but he must have some kind of spark—a bit of fire or feeling about *something*—and if he has a hint of talent, too, so much the better.

'Often he is too self-conscious to apply, or he may be tucked away somewhere in the school football team and think acting is effeminate. He may have passed unnoticed by the school producer because he can't speak correctly or doesn't look the type. Maybe his school doesn't do plays anyway, or maybe he's anti-culture and wouldn't set foot in a theatre if you paid him.

'It is young people like this who, when we find them, prove to be our most lasting members.'

With about 3,500 applicants last year, and the number increasing all the time, the auditions are conducted at five centres in Britain: London, Bristol, Birmingham, Manchester and Sunderland. Each applicant is notified of the date, time and place of his audition in

March, before the NYT staff and members of the selection panel (all old members of the Youth Theatre) start on the Grand Tour from centre to centre. The applicant is requested to arrive at the audition with photograph, stamped addressed envelope, and prepared to recite two speeches, one from Shakespeare and one from a modern play. Technical applicants, of course, are not requested to recite any speeches. Their interview consists solely of talking to the selector about their previous experience, with a view to establishing that they can make cross-halving joints, measure wood accurately or whatever the qualifications may be. Applicants for wardrobe, or scenic design and painting are requested to bring specimen art work with them.

The auditions are completely informal; everything is done to put the applicant at his ease. The audition is, in fact, more in the nature of a friendly chat than a gruelling, nerve-racking selection process. The speeches are important in that they give the selectors a first impression of the applicant's acting ability, but more importance is attached to the interview, for here the selector gets some idea about an applicant's interests, hobbies, future aspirations, reasons for wanting to join the NYT, etc.

I can vividly remember my own first audition. On my application form I had noted that I was, at that time, a Young Conservative. One of my interviewers saw this and laughed, then raised the corner of his notepaper upon which I saw written: 'Let's go with Labour.' After I had finished my two speeches, about which I can remember very little except that I seemed incapable of moving, the interviewers gave their opinion. 'Good voice,' they said. 'Good and clear.' Recently I happened to see my original audition form where, amongst other scrawlings, varying in degrees of importance, were the words: 'Can't act for his life!'

All applicants who pass the first audition are invited back to a second interview with Michael Croft in May. These auditions—the second round—are conducted at the same five centres. The requirements are exactly the same—two speeches, one Shakespearean, one modern; the form of the interview is also just the same—one recites one's speeches, then talks with Michael Croft for seven or eight minutes.

After this, there is a most nerve-racking wait until mid-June when the final selections have been made and the letter of acceptance or rejection lands on the doormat. 'Acceptance' and 'rejection' are not truly the correct words in the context of the NYT. All applicants who get through the first audition are people whom the selection committee would like to have in the company. But, because the NYT's scope is limited, invariably some must be turned away. When one considers that of the initial 3,500 applicants, 1,000 come through to the second audition, and that the NYT's highest possible intake is only in the region of 300 young people each year, it is lamentable but unavoidable that many must be disappointed.

For the past three years the NYT has run Modern Theatre Courses alongside the normal summer productions. Participation in these courses is open only to applicants who narrowly fail to get through the second round auditions. The courses last two weeks and consist of lectures by leading figures in all aspects of theatre and television, visits to some of the most interesting productions running in London at the time, observation of NYT rehearsals, as well as exercises in improvisation, movement, make-up and voice projection. A minimal fee is asked of participants to cover the cost to the NYT of theatre seats etc., but course members as well as full production members may apply to their Local Education Authority for grant aid.

Living in London is now a rather expensive business (bed and breakfast alone at a Salvation Army Hostel costs £5 17s. a week, and travelling to and from rehearsals can easily amount to thirty shillings a week). However, most LEAs in the country are very good about awarding grants to help in this respect.

There is, unfortunately, no uniformity between LEAs in the amounts they award, so that some pay all subsistence costs, some all travelling expenses plus a subsistence allowance of so much a day, or some simply pay half the total cost of participation. Whatever the policy, however, unless a member comes under one of the few unco-operative LEAs, he is assured of some sort of financial aid, and to supplement this many members take weekend or holiday jobs.

It is unfortunate that each year there are far more applications from girls than boys, since, because the NYT still concentrates on Shakespearean productions, which offer very few female parts, the intake of girls can only be very small. On the other hand, girls interested in prop making, painting, wardrobe or administrative office work are welcomed with open arms, and it has frequently been known for a girl to work in the office one year, and get a part in one of the productions the next. Movement between departments has always been easy for both boys and girls. The NYT's Regional Organiser and General Manager, David Wright, recounts: 'I joined the Youth

Michael Croft talks to the cast of Julius Caesar, *1960. Picture includes Simon Ward, Neil Stacey, Giles Block, Martin Jarvis and Michael York.*

Theatre for its modern dress production of *Julius Caesar* at the Queens Theatre. By the opening night I was, I thought, turning into an interesting double of policeman and loyal government soldier. To my surprise this passed unnoticed by the critics, and it began to dawn on me that perhaps acting was not for me.'

He became a technician, and in this capacity he happily remained until he joined the full-time staff.

New members are usually asked to be in London by a set date towards the middle of August. On this date the NYT holds its general meeting, often the only occasion during the whole season when the entire company meets together. Here the new members are introduced to the staff, start to meet older members, and are given the final details concerning the season. Since 1963 the Inner London Education

Authority have provided free rehearsal facilities in the Haverstock Secondary School at Chalk Farm, North London. It is here, in one of the two, huge gyms, that Michael Croft welcomes and addresses the assembled company.

It is exceptional indeed for a new member to be given a speaking part in his first year. Usually new members go straight into the armies (if armies feature in the productions—and usually they do since this is an ideal way of accommodating a large number of members), or into crowds of citizens *(Coriolanus)*, fair-goers *(Bartholomew Fair)*, or become soccer fans *(Zigger-Zagger)*. It is only after the member has joined the company that the staff start to notice whether he can *really* act. If he can, he will progress up the ladder and eventually find himself taking a lead part. Some members progress very rapidly indeed: Tony May—now a professional actor who has already played some large roles in films and television—joined the company in 1965. He immediately secured the one line, named part of Margarelon, a bastard son of Priam, in *Troilus and Cressida*. The following year he played Wick in *Little Malcolm* and the year after that saw him playing the title role in *Zigger-Zagger*.

13

Pompey's Sailors, Antony and Cleopatra, *Old Vic, 1965.*
Nigel Humphries sitting in foreground.

Harry (Nigel Humphries) with Zigger (Tony May).
Zigger-Zagger, *Jeanetta Cochrane Theatre, 1967.*

For boys progress is usually not so rapid. Some members without any great acting ability may not progress very far at all. But as long as they are prepared to come back, to take part and enjoy being with the company, they may play minor roles season after season. On the other hand, since the intake of girls is small, the girl who can act may progress very rapidly indeed. Helen Mirren—now with the Royal Shakespeare Company—joined the NYT in 1962 as a court lady. In 1964 she played Helena in *A Midsummer-Night's Dream,* and in 1965 became the NYT's sultry Queen of the Nile—Cleopatra.

But the rate at which a member progresses up the ladder, and whether he plays small or large parts, is of little real consequence in the NYT. There are no stars. A lead actor in one play may be asked to become a non-speaking walk-on in another.

For older members the season usually begins some two or three weeks before the general meeting. They receive notification of the plays which Michael Croft and the staff have chosen (often dictated by the theatres which are available) and are asked if possible to come up to London sometime in June to take part in casting auditions.

At these auditions members read for parts they would like to play, and the first, tentative cast lists are formed. If a member is unable to attend these auditions Croft will cast him at his own discretion (though it is always better for him to see how far a member has improved since the last season before he allocates parts).

Members are then asked to be in London by about the last week in July, and rehearsals begin at once with those actors who have been cast. Auditions continue, often for another three weeks, before all the plays have been successfully cast. Thus the basic structure of the play is rehearsed—the actors spending a large proportion of the time learning their lines—so that when the new members arrive in London they can be fitted easily into an already established pattern of work.

15

Normally, once the rehearsals are well under way, understudy auditions are held, to which all members, new or old, are invited, should they wish to try for an understudy part. It is in being an understudy that a new member can often demonstrate his acting potential, for after the plays have gone into performance an understudy call is given at which Croft not only ensures that each understudy is word perfect and sufficiently familiar with the moves to be able to take over at a moment's notice, but also assesses the dramatic potential of all new members in preparation for the next season.

The NYT is quite unable to provide accommodation for members and this they must arrange for themselves before the start of the season. There are students' hostels, digs and flats (one boy, I remember, used to stay at an hotel but he was very much an exception—he was generally regarded with some wonderment). For simplicity hostels are ideal, though they do tend to exert restrictions on members whose hours are likely to be rather irregular. Some members stay with friends. Most find accommodation in digs or flats.

Outside rehearsal each member is free to do exactly as he or she wishes. Croft has always believed in the self-reliance of young people and prefers not to dictate or meddle in what the members do with their free time; in this respect the NYT offers a wonderful opportunity for young people to come to terms with living—meeting and accepting responsibility as it comes—which in itself is an exercise of great value.

Pimlico children watch an early NYT rehearsal with John Stride (centre).

3 A season

Members had known for about a month that the 1967 season was to be the largest and probably the most exciting in the NYT's history. It was to consist of five plays including a European Tour, and the premiere of a new play called *Zigger-Zagger*, about which, as yet, we knew nothing. I had been unable to attend the first casting auditions in June and had asked Michael Croft to cast me, if possible, at his discretion. Secretly I hoped very much that I would be able to go on the Tour, but persuaded myself that this was extremely unlikely, and turned my thoughts to *Zigger-Zagger*.

In early June, however, I received a letter asking me if I could come up to London immediately to take part in a further series of auditions, since many parts had still not been filled. Thus, on a sunny Sunday morning I and a very close friend from my neighbouring town set off.

A broken fan belt between the M1 and M6 motorways destroyed all hopes of arriving in London in time for the audition. I had visions of spending the night on the road and not being able to continue until the next day, but we were lucky. The nearest garage happened to have just one belt of the right size which we fitted ourselves. So we arrived at 80, Eccleston Square (known to members as Eccleston) some two hours late, to find Michael Croft and Paul Hill clearing up after the auditions. Never mind, good to see us, and if we didn't mind just waiting a while we could have an audition: so they welcomed us.

Croft asked me to read Tybalt in *Romeo and Juliet;* Tybalt—the 'king of cats', the smooth and deadly duellist, nephew to the Capulets —a beautiful part to play; so I settled down to studying his lines. After a bite to eat Croft and Hill returned and I read Tybalt for them. They asked me to give them one passage again: 'Romeo, the love I bear thee can afford No better term than this: thou art a villain.' They then conferred for several moments before informing me that I had got the part of Tybalt, the implications of which took a long time to sink in. Not only was it a wonderful part, but also it entailed going on the European Tour!

My part was one of the last to be filled, but Paul Hill, who was directing *Romeo*, had not yet begun work on the blocking. Rehearsals

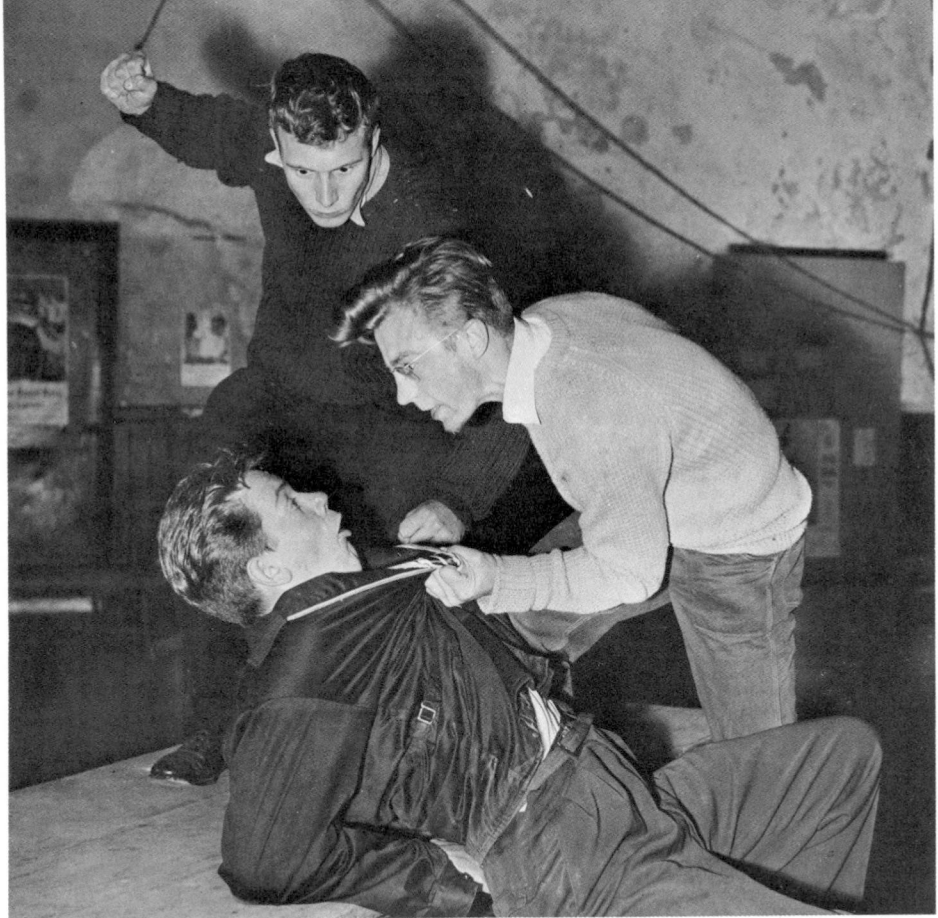

First production, Henry V, *in rehearsal, 1956.*
Pistol (David Weston) is attacked by Fluellen (Kenneth Farrington)
assisted by Gower (David Fournel).

did not start for another three days and by then, it was hoped, the
few remaining parts could be cast. Many of us spent these few days
working with the administrative staff, gradually discovering which
parts our friends had secured, and at the same time learning our lines.

In my case this was decidedly not difficult. My lines amounted to
just over thirty, so that I knew that they would not present any great
trial. The thing which did begin to dawn on me was the fact that I
had never done any serious fencing, and I had three duels to master
in the play. At school I had earned a reputation for being rather
dangerous when once let loose with a weapon, so my feelings were
mixed when I contemplated my duels.

Zigger-Zagger had already gone into rehearsal by the time the *Romeo*
cast moved up to Chalk Farm. We were still not complete, and we were
missing crowd and servants for a long time, but all the principals were

present. It was a small company in comparison to many NYT companies—there were only thirty of us in all, and most of us knew each other very well, having been members for three or four years and, in two cases, even longer. It was a happy and friendly company.

Our first job was to go through the play with our Stage Manager to take note of the cuts. As it happens there were very few. Hill was by no means adamant about cuts. If any actor badly wanted lines returned to him, and could justify his wish, they would be returned.

18

As soon as the cuts had been noted we went straight on to blocking the first few scenes. Immediately we were faced with certain difficulties which remained with us more or less throughout the rehearsal period. We had no crowd of citizens and the fights were not yet arranged, which meant that certain scenes had to remain in a most incomplete form until very near the end of the rehearsal period. Progress on the other, more straightforward scenes, however, was swift, though it is never easy to work on a flat stage area on which the ground plan is marked out by multi-coloured tapes. All too often one finds oneself walking off the front of the stage, or through solid walls, and one is never quite sure how long it will take to descend steps and so on.

The company was undertaking such a heavy programme—five plays —that this season was quite unlike any other from the very beginning. The mountain of work, especially for the directors, would have been quite impossible had it not been for the willing services of a great number of old Youth Theatre members. The Youth Theatre has what amounts to an Old Boy Network, though existing on a very different level to that which usually goes by that name; a whole host of people like Simon Ward, Jane Merrow, Martin Jarvis, John Nightingale, Geoffrey Reeves, will come back at a moment's notice to give whatever help they can, either by taking auditions or assisting on productions—in fact, anything! In 1967 Derek Seaton assisted Croft on *Zigger-Zagger* while Colin Farrell composed the music and arranged the songs for that production, and Simon Ward co-directed *Henry IV Part 1*. Even with this help, however, the season's schedule was both hectic and chaotic.

Romeo and *The Tempest* went into rehearsal simultaneously, Paul Hill, an old NYT member and professional actor, directing both productions. This meant that whilst *Zigger-Zagger* occupied one of the two gyms permanently, *Romeo* and *The Tempest* had to share the other gym and one director. Thus, for much of the season, Hill directed *Romeo* on every alternate day and the days when he was on *The*

A Rehearsal photograph. Coriolanus (John Nightingale) and soldiers prepare for battle, 1964.

Tempest our Stage Manager took rehearsals in the school dining hall, which was uncomfortably small. A very large proportion of the responsibility for the play's progress and worth therefore lay fairly and squarely on our own shoulders.

After the initial blocking of moves our rehearsals settled into a quite ordinary pattern of work. Calls for three or four days ahead would be posted and people came in as and when needed. We rehearsed the play in acts, taking the scenes in each act in sequence, working through each scene thoroughly, running it perhaps three or four times, until we reached the end of the act. Then we would run the whole act to enable the director to see how well each scene melted into the next. This, again, was made awkward by the fact that we had no scenery or scene changers as yet (who would also become crowd, servants, etc.). Since all new members were going to be required for either crowd in *Zigger-Zagger* or soldiers in *Henry IV*, which would both be running at the same time as *Romeo,* Paul Hill had to look to *The Tempest* for *Romeo's* minor characters. Caliban became a servant—Sampson—in *Romeo.* Miranda was a wench in the crowd and a dancing lady in the ball scene alongside *The Tempest's* ASM. One new member found his way into *Romeo,* and another boy on the administrative staff was persuaded to become a scene changer *cum* servant *cum* crowd, acting, I think, for the first time in his life!

For the first week of rehearsals I felt myself almost hanging in a limbo. Certainly I could deliver my lines—all thirty of them—but since nearly all my part consisted of sword fights, upon which we had not yet made a start, all I could do was wave my arms in the air and look despairingly at the director. Then, at last, Ian McKay made his first appearance of the season.

Ian McKay is an actor, fight arranger for stage and film, master swordsman—proficient with nearly every weapon one might care to mention—and has arranged the fights for the NYT since 1964.

On the first morning he called a gathering of all the fighting men in the play—servants in the first scene plus duellists—and spent the morning talking to us on and around the text. There were a great number of technical terms in the lines—'the immortal passado', 'the punto reverso', 'the hai!'—which he explained to us. At the same time he gave a comprehensive history of duelling and duellists' weapons, so that we should have a clear idea of the customs and traditions of the art and have a better understanding of the play's action. It was a fascinating history lesson, but it also helped me to a far better understanding of Tybalt's character than I had previously had. This was also true for Mercutio who has the key speech in which Tybalt is described: 'He fights as you sing pricksong—keeps time, distance, and proportion; rests me his minim rest—one, two, and the third in your bosom: the very butcher of a silk button . . .'

Only Romeo had had any previous experience with a foil; the rest of us were complete novices. McKay had brought his own practice foils with him and that day he gave us what would normally be his first twelve fencing lessons in three hours. Of course, there was no need for us to become proficient swordsmen; we had simply to learn how to handle the weapon, with the basic stances, moves, parries, thrusts, etc. This was the groundwork; necessary in order that we shouldn't appear absurd on stage. When McKay departed he left his foils behind enabling us to spend our free time until he came again practising these basic moves.

A scene in the National Youth Theatre Workshop.

Free time, I found, however, was a rare commodity. Having my car with me meant that I was mobile, and there was always someone, usually on stage management, with an urgent need to go somewhere . . .

'Simon, you wouldn't be free just now, would you?'

'What for?'

Chris Smith, the Stage Director, looking hopeful, 'I've got to go to the workshop . . .'

'Come on, hop in.'

Our workshops were situated, until recently, in Dulwich, south London. Then, a year or two ago, we found workshop accommodation not far from Chalk Farm. Here girls in paint-smeared jeans and shirts daub paint over parts of a set out in the yard. Within the building power-drills and saws make speech impossible. Frames for flats lie across the floor having the hessian stretched taut over them, others are being sized. Someone descends the ladder from the prop department upstairs clutching a huge, crested shield, the blazoning still wet. Chris Lawrence, the NYT's designer, breaks away from Chris Smith.

'Good, that's good'—the shield gets his approval—'keep at them.' He heads off towards the Master Carpenter, Chris Smith following patiently. They pore over ground plans and sheets of specifications, shouting to one another over the racing power tools. There is the

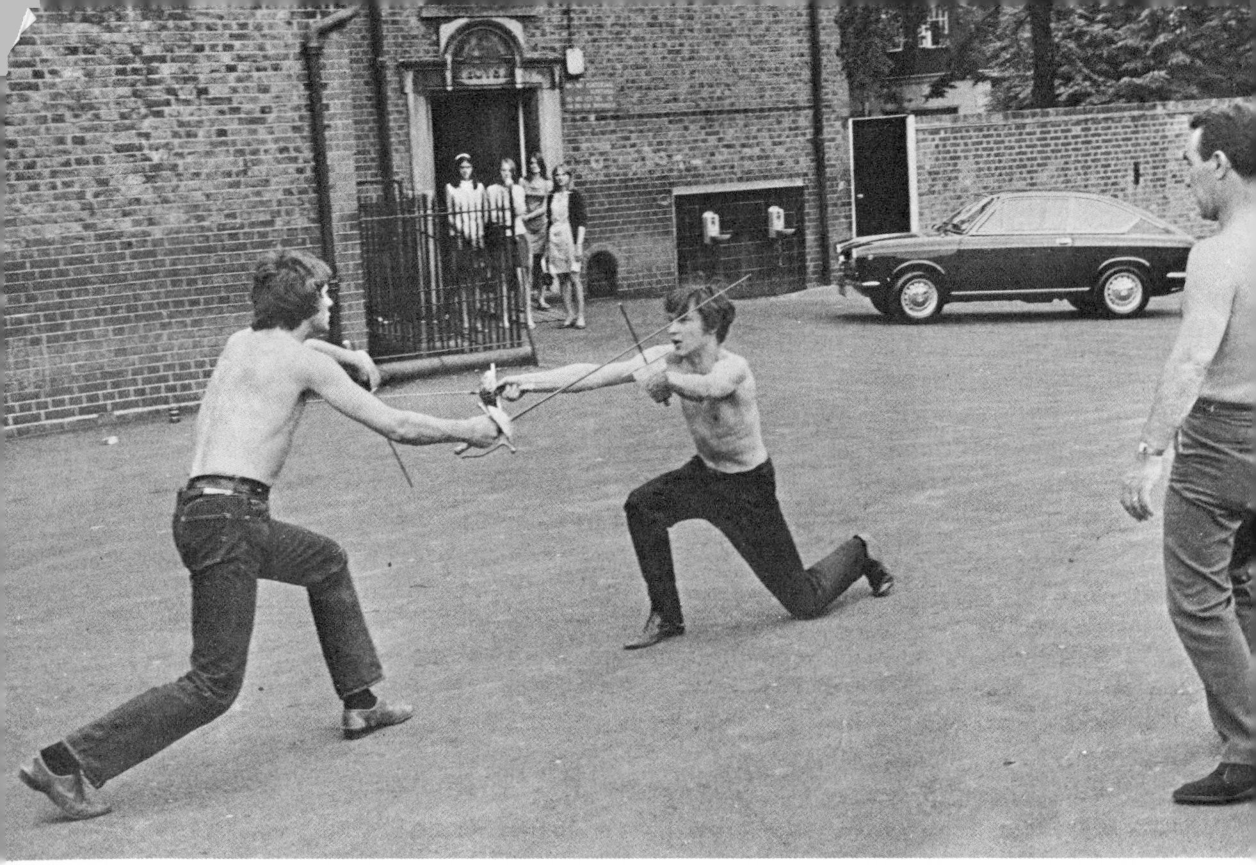

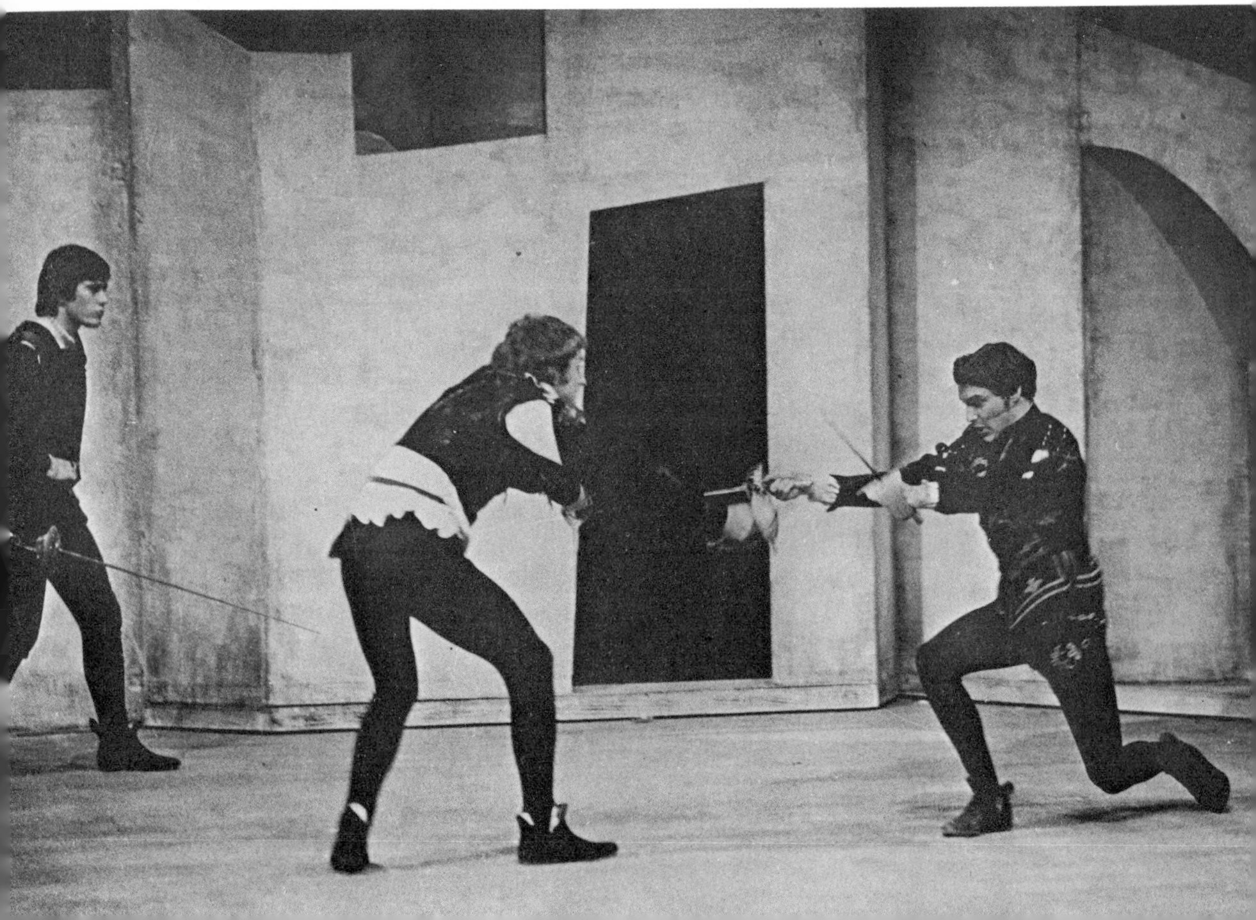

smell of wood and paint, size and sweat. Here, it seems, there is a greater intensity of activity than one could find around Haverstock School, but it is understandable since these thirty-odd technicians have to produce five sets and five lots of props in an ever-decreasing period of time. The atmosphere never changes; the workshop is always a frenzy of activity.

When McKay came next to rehearsal he immediately set about arranging the servants' fight in the first scene. Theirs was a clumsy contest of strength, with heavy, flat-bladed swords used to slash and chop. Mercutio, Romeo and I were to use epées and daggers (an epée being a type of rapier). Since the last duel between Romeo and Paris had to be very swift and not hold up the action they were to fight with rapiers alone. As soon as the servants' fight was complete and Benvolio and myself had been incorporated into the action it was possible for us to rehearse that first scene fully. So the beginning of the play took shape.

McKay immediately turned to my own duel with Mercutio. The duels consisted of several sections, each containing three or four moves. McKay would demonstrate one section for us and supervise us as we tried it, then he would go on to the next section. We would rehearse each part until we knew it perfectly and had achieved a smooth flow, gradually joining the sections together until we had one fast, unbroken duel. We inserted the 'punctuation' last of all—those fleeting pauses before each renewed attack.

After Ian McKay's first appearance at Chalk Farm, whatever free time I might have had disappeared entirely, for when I was not actually rehearsing in the gym, or racing around London with stage management staff—to the workshop, to Eccleston, to Wig Creations, to pick up a consignment of props and so on—I was rehearsing my fights. It had been impressed upon us that we could not practise them too often for they had to become second nature to us. It is possible for an actor to 'dry' in the middle of a fight, just as in the middle of his lines, only in a fight it could be most dangerous and probably far more obvious. My duel with Romeo eventually consisted of seven sections and about twenty-five moves, and was probably the most exhilarating and enjoyable experience I have had on stage. (I was also able to fulfil my long cherished ambition—to die on stage.)

As the season progressed and an arranger was brought in to choreograph the nymphs' and reapers' fertility dance in *The Tempest*, sunny days brought a remarkable spectacle in the school yard. While the

omeo and Juliet, *1967.*

*omeo (Trevor Adams) and Tybalt (Simon Masters) rehearse with
ht arranger, Ian McKay, at Haverstock School.*

he duel on stage watched by Benvolio (Richard Knott).

Romeo duellists clashed blades, the nymphs and reapers danced and gyrated to the amusement and amazement of passers-by. What on earth were all these strange young people doing?

By now new items were appearing almost daily from the workshop: furniture, wicker baskets with fruit and vegetables for the crowd street-vendors, goblets, tankards, jugs, masks for the ball scene, Juliet's tomb, plus the duellists' own specially constructed epées, and so on. By now, also, the pace of life was speeding up; rehearsals were becoming more intense, the hours longer, each company facing that awful deadline, the opening night . . .

24

*   *   *

First year members have been in London for a fortnight; older members are now in their fifth week of the season. Paul Hill is due to direct *Romeo* today; it is 10.10 a.m. He has called acts one and two for the morning and early afternoon, certain particularly bad scenes for the late afternoon, and a run of the entire play for the evening.

In the bright sun outside in the yard *Romeo* duellists are rehearsing, watched by various people from the Modern Theatre Course and *The Tempest* cast. From within the *Zigger-Zagger* gym comes an explosion of song made by over seventy swinging soccer fans. Hill has not yet arrived. No one is unduly surprised for there was a production meeting lasting into the early hours the previous night; all too often both he and Croft are unavoidably detained.

In the rehearsal gym people read old newspapers, books, scribble letters and talk. The company's ASM consults her clip board, then calls for attention.

'Quiet, please! I think we ought to start and get things moving. Can someone call everyone in from outside?'

The duellists are brought in and the company awaits the ASM's instructions. After a consultation with Romeo and Mercutio she announces that they'll run the 'Queen Mab' scene in Act I. The actors take their places and the scene is set up.

'Can everyone be quiet please . . .?'

Silence falls. Romeo: 'What, shall this speech be spoke for our excuse . . .' so the day's rehearsal begins. Outside, Paul Hill's car draws into the school yard. In the gym he finds Mercutio at the height of poetic fancy. He watches for several minutes then stops the run. He apologises for being late, then consults his call schedule to see

NYT Staff 1968. Left to right: David Wright (General Manager), Brian Croft (Technical Director), Michael Croft (Director), Paul Hill (Assistant Director) and David Fournel (Secretary).

that he's running the first two acts. 'Act I scene one.' Time hasn't been wasted but the schedule has been upset and now he must try to catch up or the whole day will be affected.

The ASM swiftly sets up the new scene. Outside an NYT truck arrives from the workshop with the *Romeo* Stage Manager plus several technicians aboard. As they start to unload props and furniture the Stage Manager enters the gym to inform Hill that they've got the servants' bucklers (small shields), lanterns and more furniture. The rehearsal is held up for a further ten minutes as people race out to help bring in the new items, adding to the already healthy stockpile of props at the back of the gym. The SM discusses various problems he has discovered at the workshop with Hill, and makes notes of specifications. The technicians finish unloading and depart.

11 a.m.: the rehearsal proper starts.

The first scene is run without stopping. It has been well rehearsed by now and there is little more Hill wishes to do with it. At the end his notes are all to do with the text. Both Hill and Croft pay fastidious attention to the text and require of every actor, however minor his role, absolute accuracy of line; whatever weaknesses the NYT may suffer through lack of experience, age and maturity, strict observance of the text is one way in which the company can shine.

So the morning's rehearsal continues, Hill quietly pacing before his desk, often not watching the actors but simply listening, while those of the cast not involved at any one time either watch quietly or drift noiselessly out till they are needed. Most remain, reading, checking lines, writing letters, not knowing exactly when this scene will finish; if the Director has to send people in search of missing actors time is wasted which cannot be afforded. There must, however, be silence during rehearsal; the passing traffic is always there but the added distraction of idle chatter in the room destroys concentration.

Hill has finished his notes on Act I by 12.40 p.m., and decides to break the company until 2 p.m. The cast stream out of the gym to join the sunbathers, and filter off to the ice-cream parlour, the cafés, or, in the case of older members, to the Enterprise, the nearest pub where there's a mad dash for the dartboard, and pints of bitter wash Cornish pasties and cheese rolls down dry throats. Here members of different casts exchange their news and compare notes. There are jokes and laughter. Twelve people endeavour to play 'killers', including three girls who are too short-sighted to see the dartboard. They don't mind being objects of fun—it's all good natured.

By 2 p.m. the hordes have returned to rehearsal, rested, reinvigorated. It's hotter now. Since Paul Hill hasn't yet returned most of the cast stay outside and sunbathe, watching the exotic ritual of nymphs and reapers. Members of the Modern Theatre Course drift back in dribs and drabs through the school gates heading for the main school block where the Course is run. *Romeo's* ASM comes hurrying across the yard from Wardrobe which is also housed in the main school block.

'Costume fitting this afternoon,' she says. 'Can I have your attention, please? I'll put a list of calls up on the board. Do have a look to make sure when you're wanted, please.'

So, as the afternoon's rehearsal gets under way, a steady stream of people disappear to Wardrobe. The costumes have come from Stratford. Beyond the girls sewing in the sun, beyond the main wardrobe room where sewing machines purr in unison, Susan Fournel and

26

In the wardrobe, Haverstock School, 1968.

Christine Lawrence, the NYT's two longstanding wardrobe mistresses, welcome each newcomer.

'Hello, who are you . . .? Yes, I know, sorry love, what character are you playing?'

'Ah, this is yours. Over there and slip it on, please,' Chris says whilst Sue searches to find adequate footwear.

'You'll have to have your hair cut.'

'Oh, can I do it?' Sue asks, and the member wonders whether to trust the eager gleam in her eyes. (From personal experience I can say that the wardrobe girls have universally proved excellent barbers, but to have three of them cutting one's hair simultaneously is not a good idea!)

Sue and Chris check over the costume to see if it needs to be taken in or let out, and whether any mending is necessary.

Back in rehearsal things are becoming more hectic. They have finished Act II, but Hill is desperately unhappy with it, and is taking each scene in the act again, separately, constantly trying to impress upon the cast the significance of the 'Italian temperament' which allows such violence to flare suddenly in the balmy, sucking heat of Verona's sun-drenched streets. Time is slipping away and there is a sense of greater urgency and intensity pervading the cast. Scenes are run four, or even five times.

6.15 p.m.—the run of the entire play is scheduled for 7 p.m.—'We'll run Act II from beginning to end,' Hill says. 'It's up to you whether you get out for food before the run.' The Stage Manager and ASM set up the first scene at the double. Outside, members of *The Tempest* cast are departing to the Swiss Cottage swimming baths. Members of the Modern Theatre Course pour out of the school to eat before going on to a show that evening. From within the *Zigger-Zagger* gym there can still be heard occasional eruptions into song.

In the fading warmth the *Romeo* cast run Act II. Hill, seated at his desk, watches silently, intently. When the act is finished he rises, glances to the clock, and informs the cast that he wants them all back promptly at 7.15, then passes through to the other gym to confer with Croft. The cast breath a small sigh of relief before hurrying away to find food.

7.10 p.m.: after a period of strange quiet and emptiness, the Chalk Farm gym is occupied once more by thirty subdued actors and actresses. The Stage Manager is setting up Act I scene one. At 7.14 precisely Paul Hill enters the gym.

'Is everyone in?'

The ASM slips outside to see that there is no one still lingering in the yard, while the cast settle on the chairs at the back of the gym.

'Everyone's in, Paul.'

He glances to the gym clock and arranges his notepaper; he is grave and quiet. Very briefly he explains that he wants this run to be treated as if it were in the theatre. He wants to see the very best they can do. He isn't going to stop it at all; simply watch.

The beginners move into position as Hill settles at his desk. The Stage Manager takes a note of the time, then the Prologue sweeps forward: 'Two households, both alike in dignity . . .' and the run has begun.

It is awkward in the gym. There is no wing space, making mass entrances difficult, so that they tend to be confused. The scene changes are bad and hold up the flow of the play because there is, as yet, no scenery and the actors are using token items like gym benches. But the play does manage to hold together and not become too disjointed.

Paul Hill rehearses Trevor Adams. Romeo and Juliet, *1967.*

Hill watches especially those scenes upon which he has spent so much time today, and to see how far the whole play has progressed since he last saw it in its entirety. He must see how much work the cast have put in on their own while he has been working on *The Tempest*. He is taking notes almost continuously.

It is a quarter past ten by the time the run finishes and Romeo, Juliet and Paris regain life. As the cast draw their chairs nearer to Hill he consults the Stage Manager over the running time of the play.

'Far too long,' is his immediate comment. 'You must cut it down, snap up the pace, cut at least eight minutes off. It drags!' Although, perhaps, everyone was expecting this and knew it in their bones already, a feeling of deflation sets in. Hill arranges his copious notes into order while people make themselves as comfortable as they can after nearly three hours on canvas chairs and, wilting, settle to listen.

'It isn't good enough,' he begins; he had found himself watching and listening to the same mistakes that had occurred a week previously; the number of textual errors means that people haven't been working on their parts outside rehearsal; it's shocking. What is the point in giving notes now if in a week's time the same mistakes are still there. He's wasting his time if people aren't going to take the trouble to work properly. *The Tempest* opens in a little over a week, he says, which means that he'll have to devote all his time over the next week to that production. The *Romeo* company will have to apply itself to work on its own, and it will require an enormous amount of hard work to make the finished product worth while and watchable. He dismisses the company.

The ASM rises swiftly and begs everyone to consult the call schedule for the next day to see when they're wanted, since there have been several changes in the calls. The company starts to trickle out of the gym into the dark, and the day's work is over.

*   *   *

We deserved Paul Hill's rebukes. After his comments we had, for the first time in my NYT experience, a lines' rehearsal, when the whole company turned up at Eccleston and ran the play, simply speaking the lines while our ASM followed them in the book and corrected us. We had no reason to feel too proud of ourselves just then.

Life became busier each day that passed; now we were entering the last frenzied stage of the season and our time outside rehearsal was always full if we wished it to be so. *Zigger-Zagger* left Chalk Farm to move into the Jeannetta Cochrane Theatre a fortnight before *Romeo* was due to open.

Now, with a play going into performance, our publicity activities also had to be intensified. The summer is always a bad time to find audiences in the West End, so each year, in what has become the great Youth Theatre tradition and spirit, members visit all the large hotels, the youth hostels and the libraries, distributing posters; they travel the tubes pressing pamphlets on to London fellow passengers; they work the West End cinema queues handing out leaflets . . .

Rehearsals finished for the day, eleven or twelve members would pile into two cars—both covered by *Zigger-Zagger* and *Tempest* posters—and head across London to Eccleston, there to pick up a large consignment of leaflets; then off again, heading for Piccadilly.

On the Eros island we would divide the leaflets amongst ourselves and disappear in pairs up the main thoroughfares.

'Everyone meet back here in three-quarters of an hour,' and we'd be off: Shaftesbury Avenue, Regent Street, Charing Cross Road, Piccadilly itself . . .

'Excuse me, sir, would you care to take one of these leaflets . . . The National Youth Theatre playing *Zigger-Zagger* at the Jeannetta Cochrane. It was especially written for us. Opens tomorrow evening at the Jeannetta Cochrane . . . do go . . .'

31

'*Zigger-Zagger*, don't miss it . . . Jeannetta Cochrane.'

'*Zigger-Zagger*, it's a great play, specially written for us . . . The National Youth Theatre . . . me? I'm a member, yes . . . you'll see it's running for four weeks. Please try to go . . . no, I'm not in it . . . and then there's *The Tempest* and *Henry IV* at the Scala . . . no I'm not in either of those, do go, especially *Zigger-Zagger* . . . no I'm in *Romeo and Juliet*. Remember, opening tomorrow at the Jeannetta Cochrane . . . no *Romeo*'s playing out of London . . .'

And then, when we ran out of leaflets we'd retrace our steps to retrieve all those which had been discarded and were littering the pavements, and start distributing them again—back towards the mad tumult of Piccadilly Circus. We'd feel exhilarated and stupidly happy, although the day had been a long, hard one. Perhaps only five per cent or less of the people we had approached would actually go to the productions, but at least there would be some. We would gather on Eros and linger a while to catch our breath, decide that food was the order of the moment and head off in search of a meal.

When *Zigger-Zagger* opened, however, it received such unprecedented, universal rave notices that there was never any doubt about its securing an audience. *Zigger-Zagger*'s success also had a strange side-effect—in that it made the *Romeo* company begin to pull together, for the rest of us realised that we had a great challenge on our hands to make the other plays live up to the acclaim which *Zigger-Zagger* was achieving.

Unlike other years we were still rehearsing *Romeo* and *Henry IV Part 1* when the summer holidays for the pupils at the Haverstock Secondary School came to an end. This meant we had to move out of the school to find other rehearsal accommodation. The school made another gym on the Maitland Park Estate, not far from Haverstock Hill, available to us. *Romeo* immediately moved in.

The move was awkward since we had to take all props and furniture

Zigger-Zagger, 1967. Bus Conductor (Loftus Burton),
Girls on Bus (Pauline Maynard and Sally Sagoe).

with us. Again I found myself up to the hilt in the operation.

On one of my several trips to Wardrobe, Christine Lawrence re-
marked, with suitable casualness, that they had to move all the
skips to the Scala Theatre where *The Tempest* would be opening in
just a day or two. Robin Fournel was to bring his Land Rover to take
care of transport, but extra hands would be very welcome to help

NYT Technicians en route, 1966.

with the loading and unloading, and no doubt my car would come in useful!

By 10.30 next morning Robin had not arrived, already half an hour late. The skips were waiting loaded, but were far too large to fit into my car. Still, abiding by the NYT's creed that no time shall be wasted I happily discovered that *Romeo*'s ASM needed to slip over to the workshop . . . 'It'll not take long . . .' She was as good as her word and we were back at the school by eleven, to find Robin had arrived with a three-ton truck; his Land Rover had broken down.

Between us we managed to fill every inch of space in the truck with the huge skips plus *Romeo* and *Henry* props, and even then there were some things left over which had to go in the boot of my car. 11.30 a.m. saw us on our way to the Maitland Park gym, hoping and praying that the back doors of the truck wouldn't burst open and spew all the contents on to the road. At the gym we off-loaded all the props, and then headed for the Scala Theatre. Ignoring the rather ludicrous, 'Strictly No Parking' signs, we stopped immediately outside the stage-door to begin the long, hard haul of off-loading the skips and hauling them up the six flights of narrow steep stairs to the Wardrobe room which was on the third floor. Since, what with our tripping up the steps, getting skips jammed or letting them slip back down the steps, banging our heads on the fire buckets and generally maiming ourselves in the process, it was two o'clock by the time we had the last skip installed, we felt quite justified in taking a short lunch break before continuing to the final port of call with the last two skips.

At headquarters we found a hive of activity comparable to that at the workshop. Girls were hurriedly stuffing envelopes; the Regional Organiser was desperately trying to make an important phone call above the row as we barged in with an immense skip and planted it in the middle of his office. In the front room our tape recording experts were trying to piece together the *Tempest* music, surrounded by yards and yards of knotted, tangled magnetic tape . . . as Michael Croft says, 'It's a near miracle that we manage to put these plays on at all!'

The Maitland Park gym, now containing both the *Romeo* and *Henry* props and furniture, was much darker and smaller than those at the Haverstock School, which meant that it was some time before we could accustom ourselves to this new environment.

We rehearsed only for a short while in this gym; with the arrival of the opening night of *The Tempest* we were able to have Paul Hill's undivided attention for the first time that season, so it was not too surprising that the production did begin to regain its sparkle.

Slight problems had been arising over the sound cues, especially the music for the dance sequence at the Capulet's ball. Hill had brought in a dance choreographer who had taught us the primary steps whilst we were still at Chalk Farm. Now, at Maitland Park, we began to put the dance to the music under the choreographer's direction.

In the short time we were at the Maitland gym our set arrived and was erected, which enabled us to see it for the first time. I, for one, realised that the ground plan had signified very little of what the set was actually like. The elevations were much higher than I had imagined, and the design of architecture most magnificent. Looking down from the highest elevation I understood why Ian McKay had had me jumping from the top wall bar of the Chalk Farm gym, sword in hand, and had then decided against my making my last entrance in this way!

We acted upon the set for about two days, running the play in its

34

entirety to sort out the scene changes and to time the scene changers' entrances with the sound effects equipment. Erecting the set at the gym had not been done specifically for our benefit, but as a trial run to see how well it worked, how long it took to erect and as a guide for the technicians who would have to put it up on the Tour. The set itself had been specially constructed to simplify the process. Its foundation was easily erectable scaffolding, on to which the flats were bolted. Each section was as large as it could be, taking into account that it had to be small and light enough to be carried and lifted by two or three men; and it had to be possible to pack the whole set plus props and furniture into one truck.

35

Upon our eviction from the Haverstock School, Croft had taken *Henry IV* to rehearse at Eccleston which proved far too small for that large production. It was agreed, therefore, that *Romeo* should move again, and that *Henry IV* should take over the Maitland Park gym. We were consequently informed that *Romeo* was to rehearse on the Jeannetta Cochrane stage during the morning, as well as those afternoons when there was no *Zigger-Zagger* matinee. Perhaps a small groan did emerge from the cast, but we were becoming used to being

Barrie Rutter (centre) rehearsing as Falstaff,
Henry IV Part 1.

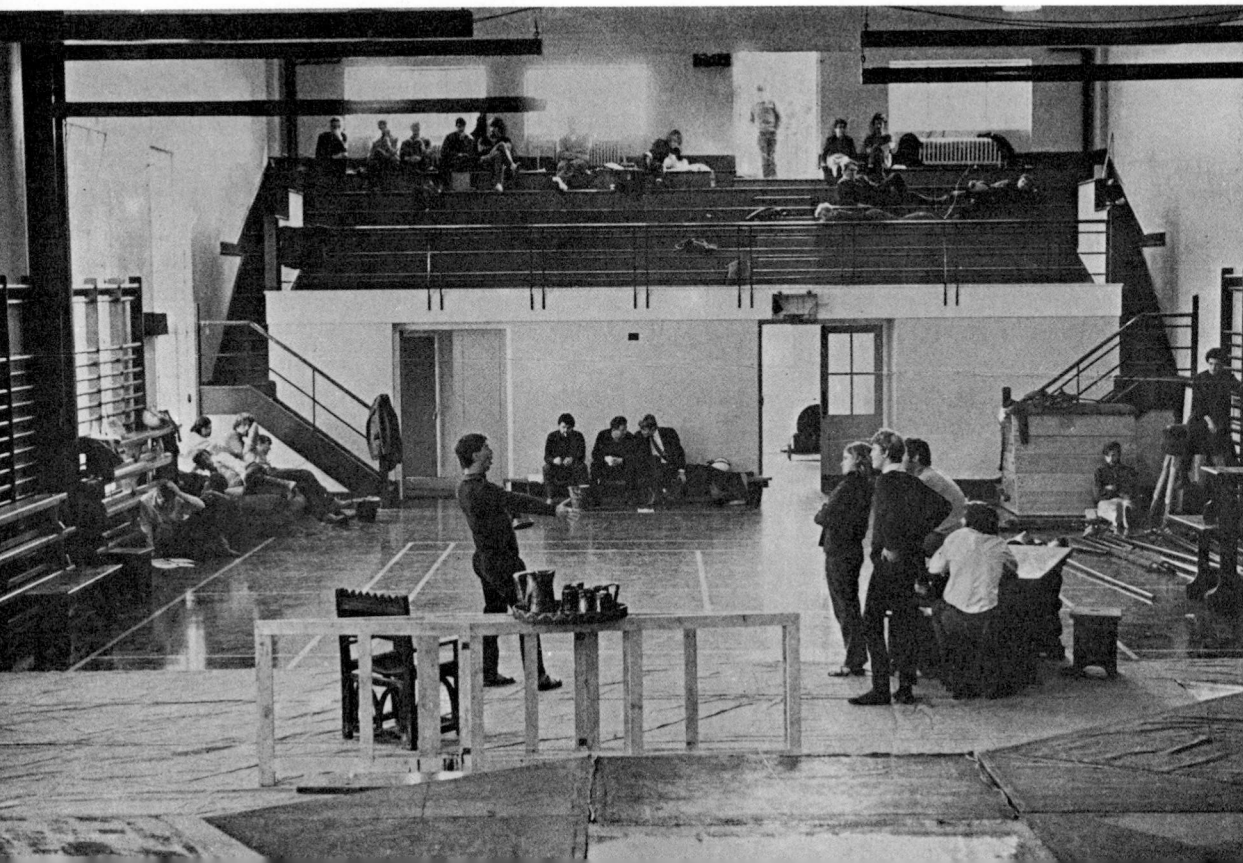

gypsies by this time. Happily, however, the move turned out to be one of the best things that could have happened to the company.

I can well remember that first morning we moved to the Jeannetta Cochrane. Until this time I had been carrying the *Romeo* swords and daggers in my car boot for safety, but my car had broken down yet again and was in a garage for the day, and thus I found myself on the upper deck of a London Transport bus with a tidy little armoury rolled up in a sleeping-bag beneath my arm, which clashed and rasped most alarmingly each time I moved. However, I did manage to reach the Cochrane without being arrested for the possession of offensive weapons.

The *Zigger-Zagger* set consisted of a scaffolding stand which towered at the back of the stage, on which the football crowd sat, cheered, yelled and sang during performance. With a little imagination we were able to pretend that it was our own set, since it provided the necessary elevations which we were able to adapt for *Romeo*.

As soon as the company got on stage a change took place. Everything seemed much more real, the atmosphere so much more stimulating, that the play suddenly regained its life and energy. It was as if the exciting and vitally tumultuous spirit of *Zigger-Zagger* had entered us through our occupation of the Cochrane, investing us with new determination. In the last week of rehearsal Hill spent most of the time running the play from beginning to end, then picking out the bad scenes and thoroughly working them over. In the short time we were at the Cochrane the play was transformed. From a dead, slow performance it became fast, sparkling, and full of life. The morale of the whole company lifted, and at last it looked as though we should have a successful production on our hands.

East Grinstead is about an hour and a quarter's coach journey south-east of London. The Adeline Genée, named after a famous ballerina, is a very new, comfortable little theatre seating about four hundred, about a mile out of the town. This was to be our launching pad for the Tour. Croft had decided to play *Romeo* out of London to keep it separate from the actual London season, so we were to treat the Genée as our first date of the Tour. Our week's run was aimed at providing us with a good chance to smooth out all the problems which we might discover in performance before actually going abroad, so that we would set off with a production which would be as near technically perfect as possible.

Since our theatre was so far away from the company's lodgings and

37

Barrie Rutter plays Falstaff, 1967.

digs in London a coach was laid on each day to take us to and from the theatre. (We were to spend a very large proportion of the next three weeks in a coach!)

The set moved into the Genée on Saturday the ninth of September. The fit-up lasted well into the night. The company followed it in on the Sunday for a technical run and costume parade. Paul Hill had worked through the night lighting the play himself, and had had only four hours sleep in the theatre stalls!

38

A typical get-in.

The coach was late in arriving at the theatre, putting the schedule off its timing. Croft travelled down from London to personally supervise the costume parade which we held straight away.

The technical run eventually began after our sandwich lunch, and it dragged on through the afternoon and early evening. Here boredom cannot be avoided; for the Director and technical staff as well as the actors, who have spent a month or more rehearsing the play and come into the theatre at last, it is frustrating to have to crawl through the performance in full costume and make-up, stopping frequently for the pan to be sorted out, for a scene change to be rearranged, for a new lighting cue to be worked out. But all this is essential. Without the technical rehearsal the play would probably run into a hundred unforeseen difficulties.

39

Late on Sunday evening the company returned to London exhausted. We were able to sleep in on Monday morning, however, since our call at the theatre was not until the afternoon. Then, in an unusually calm fashion, the company ran a Dress Rehearsal which promised well for that night. We were able to rest once more before the curtain rose at 7.15 p.m.

Our opening night coincided with that of *Henry IV Part 1* which had taken over from *The Tempest* at the Scala. Our first night was, in fact, quite uneventful, except that the play went well, was received well, and gave us a good start to the run. As always, with an audience present for the first time to give our nerves that edge of tension, we improved enormously on the Dress Rehearsal.

Our week at the Genée was unspectacular. We had full houses each night, with very little variation in the type of audience or in their reaction to the play. But it was a successful week in that it served its purpose. Previously unforeseen snags were discovered and ironed out.

As soon as we had arrived at the theatre and got into costume the other duellists and I discovered that our boots slipped on the stage cloth, which would make the duels exceedingly dangerous considering that we were using untipped weapons. There were two ways of remedying this; either by putting resin on to the cloth, or by sticking rubber soles and heels on to our boots. Due to the shortage of time the stage management staff decided upon the latter treatment and provided us with rubber soles. They did not immediately secure us rubber heels, and it wasn't until after the second night that the real necessity for heels became apparent.

D

Towards the end of my duel with Mercutio, as Romeo dashed between us to stop our fight and I made the fatal lunge at Mercutio, my heels slipped on the cloth. Instead of aiming my blade beneath Mercutio's arm I stabbed him hard in the stomach as I fell, and he doubled up in all too realistic pain. Desperately trying to regain my feet I struggled on the floor. Romeo drew his own sword and made several ineffectual lunges at me, then caught hold of my arm as I stumbled towards the wings so that I was dragging him after me. I fell into the wings shaking, and furious with myself. Then Romeo slipped on his heels and collapsed half on, and half off stage.

Ruefully rubbing his stomach Mercutio advanced to the front of the stage and delivered his next line: 'I am hurt . . .' The audience found it impossible to contain its mirth. For the next performance we all had rubber sticker heels on our boots.

The production remained principally as Hill had rehearsed it. During the week we managed to cut several minutes off our running time as we became more confident, and we kept up a pleasingly high, level standard of performance. The reviews which appeared in the local Press were all good.

While we were appearing at the Genée, Croft and Hill joined forces in London to direct *Henry V,* the last of the season's productions destined for the cold lands of the north—Sunderland. We were unable to see anything of that production, though we heard incredible stories of its instant creation much later. *Henry IV Part 1* was playing to full houses of school parties, and it seemed that, with the continuing success of *Zigger-Zagger*, everything one could have hoped for had been achieved.

But for me one of the most satisfying moments of the whole season was on our last night at the Genée. It was Friday the fifteenth of September. The next day both *Zigger-Zagger* and *Henry IV Part 1* ended their runs, and for those casts the season was almost over. For us, however, there was none of the last night blues. We had a two-week European Tour still to look forward to. In a rather strange way it seemed that our real season was only just beginning!

Tybalt (Simon Masters on floor)
s killed by Romeo (Trevor Adams)
ith Benvolio (Richard Knott)
watching. Romeo and Juliet, *1967.*

4 The National Youth Theatre abroad

The NYT first went abroad in 1960, touring Holland with *Hamlet*; there have since been seven further visits to the Continent, with another visit to the Berlin International Festival to come in the immediate future. Of all these foreign trips one stands out like a very sore thumb—the tour of Italy in 1961, the ITALIAN CAMPAIGN!

I heard about this tour in my very first season. It has become part of the Youth Theatre legend, a story passed on from old members to new like folklore, except that it cannot be distorted or exaggerated through the passage of time; the truth is too tragi-comic for invention to be possible.

The 1960 *Hamlet* tour of civilised Holland had gone so well and so smoothly that possibly Croft had been lulled into a false sense of optimism. When *Julius Caesar* in modern dress opened at the Queen's Theatre, London, the NYT's reputation and prestige was immeasurably enhanced by the play's enthusiastic critical reception. As a result, Croft received an invitation from an Italian Theatre Club to take the production on a tour of Italy in April 1961, which, after the success of the Dutch tour, appealed to him. He felt also that it would be an exceptionally valuable educational experience for the company.

There were small problems from the outset (small in comparison to the problems which were to come) which made Croft cut his budget, until he realised that the NYT would in any case make a loss on the tour, and that members would have to pay a proportion of their accommodation costs—which they gladly agreed to do. However, impressed by the enthusiasm of the Italian arrangers who had now enlisted the help of the British Council and secured the patronage of Signora Gronchi, the Italian President's wife, he was willing to go on.

As April drew nearer, however, the problems began to grow larger and more serious in connection with the contract, payment, and arrangements for the tour; and with the scenery truck due to depart for Italy on April fifth, April fourth found Croft dispatching 'last warning' telegrams and threatening to call the whole thing off if the contractual disagreements were not settled; they were settled at the last moment and the truck departed.

Here it is worth while to depart from the main narrative and let Brian Croft (no relation to Michael Croft), the tour's Stage Director, relate a few of the incidents which plagued the technical staff. Having had to cram himself, three other technicians and a West End set into a 15 cwt. van and a shooting-brake, due to the stringent budget, he was thus prepared to follow Hannibal:

'On the first day we managed to overheat the engine on the white cliffs of Dover. Thirty kilometres south of Boulogne we exploded a front tyre on the van and snapped a spring in the process. A hundred-mile diversion via Paris, driving overnight, saw the spring replaced. Another all-night drive to Lyons and we were back on schedule. However, we took different routes out of the town and spent the rest of the day looking for each other on a sun-baked seventy mile strip of the Route National Seven. Finally, both vehicles gave up the search and we met, as if by chance, at the frontier after our third night of driving and the mirages which go with it.

'At the customs barrier we had our first taste of the Italian temperament "at work". We spent seven frantic hours battling with customs

43

Julius Caesar, *1960. Portia (Jane Merrow) and Brutus (Neil Stacey).*

officials. The required import licence had not been deposited by the Italian organisers of the tour. This was settled by half a dozen long-distance telephone calls, but officialdom was not content to leave it at that. As we were about to depart it was decided to search the over-loaded van—the back doors burst open and spewed most of the contents on to the road. We pointed out twenty times that the rifles for Mark Antony's army were dummies and that the Teddy Boys' flick-knives couldn't have been blunter. Officialdom insisted that the weapons could be lethal. Finally, after reaching a point where we were about to demonstrate how easy it would be to kill someone with our bare hands, they gave up—probably because it was time to go off duty. My documents got the stamp, the treble stamp, and we left for Florence.

'We drove all night through mountain roads, stopping only once for a puncture. Twelve hours later we scarcely noticed it when we drove the van under a low garage roof and ripped off the heavily laden roof rack; just a three-hour delay, tying it all back on.

'We arrived in Florence two hours before the company and in time to snatch three hours' sleep before starting on an all-night session in the theatre. The "balance of power" seemed to be simple. Offset disasters by sacrifice of sleep and you could maintain the all-important (almost impossible Italian-arranged) schedule. Of the actual tour these are only a few incidents still vivid in my memory.'

Owing to the late start of the performances—9.30 p.m.—the technical staff could not begin to strike the show until 12.30 a.m. (generally later). It then took them another three hours to complete the work of striking and loading the set, after which they had to start the drive to the next venue, probably over a hundred miles away, at once. On average, throughout the tour, these technicians had less than three hours sleep a night.

The opening night in Florence was a great success, and the performance was highly praised in the Florentine Press. Immediately after the performance, however, the Italian organisers *informed* Croft that at least half an hour would have to be cut from the running time, which should be brought about by cutting the long speeches of Cassius, together with the quarrel scene and that vital Brutus soliloquy: 'It must be by his death'. The time was 12.45 a.m. Croft, having been working for most of the previous night, was not in a mood to agree to any sort of proposal by that management. The Italians then informed him that unless he complied the company would not be allowed to perform at the next venue in Rome. Croft, furious and very tired, sought refuge with his stage staff in a nearby café where they remained until 2 a.m., hoping that tempers would calm in their absence.

The Italians did not give way over the cuts, but made several additional demands including lighting and costume changes. Croft decided, in the face of this absurdity, to simply ignore them and go ahead as if the argument had never arisen. The technicians had been due to arrive in Rome at eight in the morning. As it was, the scenery truck did not leave Florence until 5.30 a.m., the technicians now in their sixth day of driving or working, simply cat-napping when they could. Upon their arrival in Rome they were assailed by the Italian Management for wasting time and not arriving sooner!

In fact, following the road directions given to them by the Italians down the new autoroute, they had found that it was inexplicably closed to traffic and had had to return to Florence to find a totally different route for themselves. They arrived in Rome at 8 p.m. and went straight into the theatre where they worked solidly until 1 a.m. the next day. Five hours sleep in seventy-two hours.

The Italian technicians in Rome were notoriously slow workers. After Croft had watched three of them take nearly two hours to rig one lamp his patience ran out. He decided to supervise them himself. Nevertheless it was not until 6.30 a.m. that the setting was complete and the plotting could begin. Then, without any warning the electricians disappeared, and did not return until twelve noon. The company rehearsal which had been planned, had to be scrapped since the lighting was completed only just in time for the first performance.

There were four performances in Rome, and the lighting changed so much during the course of them that the actors were continually forced to change their acting areas, and occasionally to grope around the stage looking for some kind of light in which to play. Scenes which should have been flooded with light were given hardly any, and scenes supposed to be played with low lights were over-lit. The electricians either could not, or would not, comply with the lighting plan so that in the end both Michael Croft and Brian Croft had to stand over them on the switchboard to correct the mistakes as they happened.

On top of this the Italian organisers had decided that the use of a simultaneous translation system would bring the play to a far wider audience, to which Croft reluctantly agreed. The system worked by

45

NYT on tour. On the roofs of Copenhagen.
Alan Allkins, Neil Stacey, Michael Cadman, Michael Croft, Mary Grimes,
Giles Block, Diana Rasbach, John Nightingale.

having an Italian actor in an open box who translated the play as it
went on, and who could be heard by the audience through small
receivers which were available for hire. This created utter chaos.
The novelty of the apparatus itself led to hilarious discussion during
the performances. Some of the receivers went wrong and people
angrily and noisily protested, then barged out of their seats to com-
plain to the management. As the noise from the audience grew worse
because those people who had receivers began translating the text
to those who were without, the play was made inaudible. Meanwhile,
the Italian actor was forced to raise his voice in trying to make
himself heard, and attempting to match the dramatic tones coming
from the stage. Often, in his absorption, he would rush on in Italian,
delivering lines which had not yet been reached in English!

Not all the problems were technical by any means. The most serious
ones were due to temperament. Involved yet again in a disagreement

over payment and the terms of contract, Croft, foreseeing the cancellation of one particular performance, and the Youth Theatre's fee going completely west, agreed to a compromise with the Italian organisers. Thus the performance went ahead and ran relatively smoothly until the first interval. It then transpired that the electricians had not been paid, and it was a choice of either paying them or paying the Youth Theatre. The money had been promised to the Youth Theatre, so the electricians forcibly restrained the Stage Manager from taking the curtain up on the second half, and a wholesale brawl developed on stage, in which the management joined. While the argument swayed violently across the stage with much shouting and cursing, and the audience began a slow hand-clap of impatience, Croft and the cast were forced to stand around waiting for the violence to abate.

47

The interval lasted fifty-five minutes. That night the final curtain came down at 1.15 a.m.!

As a result of all these troubles the Italian Management arbitrarily cancelled the company's accommodation, as if to punish them. Thus, arriving in Genoa at 9.30 p.m. in a torrential downpour, they had to find their own accommodation, making on the spot arrangements, some members ending up in a quite extraordinary boarding-house. 'Educational,' they said, 'in the broadest sense of the word.'

Hamlet,
*Paris Festival,
1960.
Guildenstern
(Alan Allkins),
Hamlet (Richard
Hampton),and
Rosencrantz
(Simon Ward).*

One may wonder how, under this sort of stress, with such incredible incompetence on the part of the Italians, the company ever managed to present anything vaguely recognisable as *Julius Caesar*. In fact, the multitude of adversities knitted the sixty-four members of the company together in a spirit of unity and determination which made it possible for them to rise over and above such daunting difficulties, and for the critics to praise the productions, ironically saying that this was the best thing that this particular Italian Management had done.

It was, I suppose, almost inevitable that the long-suffering technicians should have the last awkward encounter of the tour. David Wright, one of the assistant technicians, vividly remembers their return journey: '. . . the Youth Theatre van, returning through France, loaded with a bearded Stage Director, sixty dummy rifles, several machine-guns and a bazooka, found that, with France on the verge of civil war on account of the Algerian crisis, and with paratroopers ringing Paris, this was not an easy cargo to explain away. Even after being stopped eleven times, however, and almost arrested twice, we found that de Gaulle's military was less unpleasant than our Italian Management!'

49

So ended a never-to-be-repeated chapter in the Youth Theatre's history. The company has not been to Italy again. Every tour, however, leaves behind its own fund of stories of disaster and crisis; like July 1961 at the start of the Dutch tour when Brian Croft managed to get himself wedged with a sixteen-foot portcullis in the door of the guard's van at Liverpool Street station, with the train about to pull out in three minutes. An ASM, realising that the tools were inside the van squirmed through the portcullis, seized a saw, and, by cutting the portcullis in half, liberated Brian just in time!

Or again, that lightning trip to the 1960 Paris Festival with *Hamlet*. The costumes' and props' skips were found to be too large for the airline coach, so, resourceful as ever, members flagged down a rag-and-bone truck and persuaded the driver to take the skips to the airport. There they found that the skips were too large to fit into the plane—'Discard them,' was the cry, 'carry the costumes on you . . .' So the company arrived, costumes, swords, goblets and all other props literally hanging around them, having to face a Dress Rehearsal and three performances in one and a half days.

At the 1961 Berlin Festival the company had to rehearse on a cinder football pitch and were lent a whole armoury of weapons for use in the battle scenes by the British garrison there, but had to

amlet, Paris Festival, 1960.
he duel between Laertes (John Shrapnel)
d Hamlet (Richard Hampton).
ackground: Claudius (Kenneth Farrington)
d Gertrude (Michael Butcher).

return these to H.Q. each night—loading Winchesters and Sten-guns into an army truck like midnight conspirators after each performance.

These were the stories of which the *Romeo* cast was reminded as we stood on the brink of our own European Tour. Was ours also to be chaotic and fraught with crises? The answer turned out to be a very simple 'no'.

In comparison with the Italian Campaign the *Romeo* tour was a dream. Nearly everything worked: our reception was incredible, the play miraculously improved at each performance . . . and we enjoyed every minute.

50

We left London on September seventeenth, on the train for Harwich, where we boarded a Dutch boat for what was to be a tranquil, sunny but cold six-hour crossing to the Hook of Holland. There we boarded the Rotterdam Express and soon found ourselves pulling into the magnificent Central Station. We were to be in Holland for a week, staying with private families in each town. I don't think I have said 'hello' or 'goodbye' to so many people in so short a space of time ever before!

Brian Croft and our stage management and technical staff had made the crossing earlier in the day, and our set had already arrived at the theatre, the Stadsschouwburg, or the municipal theatre (all the theatres are called Stadsschouwburg).

On Monday we were free to spend our time exploring Rotterdam, a city completely rebuilt since the war and very much like parts of Coventry, only on a much larger scale. The Stadsschouwburg had been razed to the ground during the ferocious bombing attacks on this vital port, but the city had rebuilt the theatre, as a temporary measure, using the original stones and bricks from the old building. As so often in Britain, this temporary measure had become something of a permanent feature, for the city had decided to build a new Concert Hall instead. Nevertheless, when we arrived at the theatre at 7.15 p.m. for our eight o'clock opening, we stood in awe in the vast spaces of this huge building. The back-stage area could easily have contained two very large stages, and as one stared up to the gloom overhead one could not see the roof. I could not help comparing this, my first taste of a Continental theatre, with the cramped conditions in many of London's West End theatres. During the course of the tour we were to play in even larger theatres, some of the most modern in Europe, as well as one which must be numbered among the smallest in the world. If there was any monotony in the amount of travelling we did

The Romeo and Juliet *Company leaves Liverpool Street Station for the Continent, September, 1967.*

by coach, variety was the word which described the theatres.

We had been told that our first night had to go smoothly since the Dutch national Press would be present and their reviews of the performance would go ahead of us to each of the other towns we were to visit. To follow up a bad Press would be a dismal experience, which would also affect the bookings.

When the curtain went up, though it had all the feel of a first night, I don't think any of us were particularly conscious that we were playing to a foreign audience consisting mostly of young people. That fact very swiftly made its impression, however.

We found that we were playing against a constant barrage of talking, whistling, and even shouting, an ever-growing distraction of a kind we had not really experienced in Britain. Little did we know that Rotterdam had become notorious for similar attempts to wreck performances. By the second interval it had escalated to such an extent that we decided to increase the speed of the performance to get the ordeal over as quickly as possible. Already we were sure that those good Press notices would not materialise. We could not have been more surprised in the morning when our kind hosts (all of whom spoke excellent English) read the notices to us. While the production and composure of the company was praised, the critics took up most of the space in condemning the audience for its rudeness! We were over the first hurdle.

Thereafter, though our audiences continued to consist principally of young people (which is what we wanted in any case) we encountered no more barracking, and one of the most constant features in the provincial reviews was the critics' praise for their own local young people in comparison with the unruly Rotterdam teenagers.

This was the NYT's fourth visit to Holland, and, as on the previous tours, the Dutch people extended to us the kindest hospitality and warmest reception imaginable. As the tour progressed our after-performance receptions began to become almost Beatlesque, with hordes of teenagers milling outside the stage doors through which we had to dash for the coach. Rotterdam became an amusing, distant memory. We found none of that all-too-British reserve amongst our audiences, and, after our rather staid reception in England, such exuberance was most refreshing.

Holland is split into areas, each predominated by some particular religious following, so the north is mainly Protestant, while the south, near the Belgian border, is largely Roman Catholic. We found that each area had its own customs when it came to giving applause. Our initial dismay can be imagined at the end of one performance, when we heard the audience begin a slow hand-clap—until we learned that this was their way of showing their appreciation. As we took our bows on another occasion, to our astonishment the whole audience rose and stood cheering, hands clapping above their heads. We all knew about standing ovations so we were a little deflated to learn that this too was simply a custom of the area.

With a new town, new hosts, and a new theatre each day, every performance was like another first night. We had no chance to settle into an easy routine, to become familiar with our stage and environment. To know where the stage was and how to get to it from one's dressing-room was all one had time to register and this may account for the way our performance improved during the tour. We could never stop thinking about what we were doing. The play never had a chance to become totally automatic and dead, but at the same time,

Romeo (Trevor Adam
and Juliet (Veronica Sowerby
Romeo and Juliet, *1967 tour*

52

working on every size of stage imaginable, under such differing conditions, we became exceedingly efficient at adapting ourselves, and grew more confident in our performance.

Our time in Holland was like a whistle-stop tour, leaving only vague impressions and blurred memories. We played early matinees, late matinees and evening performances. The time of day began to have less significance.

It was the custom in Holland for the first interval to be a long one, usually a quarter of an hour, and for the second to be merely a token five minutes. Before we had left England Ian McKay had given us strict instructions to rehearse our duels on stage before each performance, so that we could adapt ourselves to the size of the stage, and keep the fights fresh in our minds, and this we did, each day, in that long first interval. As far as the actors were concerned very little appeared to go wrong. I learned from our Stage Manager, some time afterwards, that things on the technical side had not been quite so smooth-running; for instance, there was the theatre where there was no connecting system between the prompt corner and the lighting box, so for each lighting cue, the Stage Manager had to give an arm signal some three minutes early to Brian Croft, who would be stationed overhead on a gantry. Croft would then race round the gantry to the lighting box and say 'Go' and the lighting change would take place . . .

Our set had been designed so that certain parts of it could be discarded when we were playing on very small stages like that at Maastricht, or the school hall—the Gymnasium Kreuzgasse—in Cologne, where I experienced my most embarrassing moment of the tour. Because the stage was so small the steps down which I made my last, dramatic entrance, were at a different angle to their normal position. I uttered my first few words: 'Thou, wretched boy . . .' started down the steps, 'that didst consort him here . . .' then slipped and travelled the rest of the way down on my backside to roars of laughter from the audience. I was especially glad to be killed and hide my shame in death that evening.

In comparison with these small stages we played in theatres which held 2,000 people, upon whose stages even our fine set seemed a little lost. Such was the Stadsschouwburg at Eindhoven—our last call in Holland. The theatre was brand new, immense and magnificent, with dressing-rooms which were palatial in comparison with those to which we were accustomed. Here, as was the case throughout the tour, we played to a full house. The idea that there were two thousand people watching and listening to us seemed almost incredible, but there they were, and their applause was real enough.

We passed across the border between Holland and Belgium without being really aware of the fact, to enter the second stage of the tour. Now there would be no more hosts, only hotels; the schedule made greater demands upon us, everything grew more hectic, and culminated in two performances in Brussels during British Week.

We travelled from Eindhoven to Antwerp where we played an evening performance, then back into the coach and on to Brussels, arriving at just before one in the morning. At 9.30 next day we left Brussels for Namur where we played a 1.30 matinee, then back to Brussels where we had the evening free to explore (vivid memories of the golden, bird market square). Away again by 8.30 the next morning en route for the German city of Cologne, a ride of nearly two hundred miles. We performed in Cologne at 6 p.m., then back into the coach and on to Frankfurt—another hundred miles. We arrived in Frankfurt at about two in the morning and were in bed within half an hour. Six hours sleep then up and off for a performance at 10.15 in the morning. We were looking somewhat haggard by this time, and were feeling none too bright since a bug had gone round the company and we were all suffering from sore throats and a kind of fever.

That morning performance in Frankfurt might have been a very dismal affair indeed, had it not been for the actual theatre. I remember vividly the coach travelling beside a railway line beyond which, about a mile away, we saw a great dome shining in the sun like a steel bubble. The coach turned over the railway track and began to head for the dome. I don't think any of us really believed that that could be the theatre—but it was. (This was where Cassius Clay fought the German champion Karl Mildenberger.)

We were late on schedule and already hordes of young people were milling about the main entrance. There seemed to be thousands of them. The dome itself consisted of steel, octagonal scales, and was the largest superstructure of its kind I have ever seen. It took us nearly five minutes to walk from the main entrance to the stage door, round the never-ending sweep of plate-glass windows through which we saw the luxurious restaurant in which we were later to be entertained by the theatre management.

The dressing-rooms were like five-star hotel rooms, with huge, deep carpets, swivelling, leather leisure chairs, low walnut tables, potted

55

E

plants, an abundance of mirrors, excellent lighting, and private toilet, showers and wash basins to each room. Our colds were forgotten.

Once again the theatre held two thousand people and we were playing to a full house. The stage afforded oceans of space, and was wired with the most efficient microphone system which Brian Croft was certain would detect a pin falling. This did bring a certain novelty to the performance since we could always hear a slight echo, but since, when one looked from the back of the steeply raked auditorium to the stage it was like looking down from the back of a football stand to the opposite goal, the microphones were very necessary.

After our meal in the theatre restaurant, we were taken on an official sight-seeing tour of Frankfurt which was arranged by our friends at the British Council, and in the evening we all went to a dance-meeting-manifestation with young people from several Frankfurt Youth Clubs, where we gyrated to the blasting sound of a local pop group.

The next day we had a leisurely drive back to Brussels, and a day in which to recuperate.

And then came the climax of the tour. In a city festooned with Union Jacks, shops loaded with British goods, red London Transport buses trundling through the streets, we were to present two performances at the Palais des Beaux-Arts.

Michael Croft and David Fournel, the NYT's secretary, both came out to see our last performance. It went exceptionally well, and at the end of this performance we received a true, standing ovation—a most fitting conclusion to a wonderful tour.

5 Important past productions

In the first chapter I said that the original NYT production, *Henry V* in 1956, received some notice from the critics at least. As the immediate successor to the remarkable series of Alleyns' productions it was still only a school play—though outside school auspices—to which the director had the audacity to invite national critics. But by doing so a measure of interest was focused on the Youth Theatre, and interest was, and still is, needed more than praise.

In the *Daily Telegraph*, W. A. Darlington gave the venture a magnificent send-off. He wrote: 'It had been my first intention to write a detached, cool, critical notice of the Youth Theatre's production of *Henry V* at Toynbee Hall last night, but now I am at my desk I find it impossible.

'The play comes over brilliantly, and one has the impression that it is a long time since one saw it more successfully cast.

'In this production Mr Croft shows publicly what he has so often shown in private, that he has a particular genius for inspiring young people to act. His whole cast works with a pleasure which is infectious, and their standard of speaking, both for precision and audibility, is most refreshingly high.'

Mr Darlington was acute in his observation. In this first production the *general* public, as opposed to uncritical school performance audiences, were offered, practically for the first time, Shakespeare played by young people bringing to their task those qualities which only youth can give.

The Times echoed Mr Darlington's enthusiasm: 'The production aroused high hopes of the artistic worth and future of the venture. It is a production of admirable simplicity, beautifully lit.'

It has been said that the English are swift to praise a new venture, but are less ready to continue their praise if that venture seems to be in danger of becoming a fixture—something solid with firm foundations. Although from the very beginning Sir Ralph Richardson, Sir John Gielgud, Peter Ustinov and Richard Burton were avid outspoken supporters of the venture—(Peter Ustinov wrote: 'A movement such

as the Youth Theatre is more than a mere step in the right direction. It will serve to focus public interest on the tremendous, spontaneous activity in the field of drama in schools, and youth clubs, and it will serve as a most necessary outlet for the enthusiasm and dramatic instincts of youth.')—it was not until 1959/60 that the company really began to capture public and critical attention to any great degree. The very fact of the Youth Theatre's survival is thanks to two productions: *Hamlet* and *Julius Caesar*.

In 1959 Michael Croft took the Youth Theatre to the Queen's Theatre in Shaftesbury Avenue for its summer productions. This was the Youth Theatre's first appearance in the West End. With typical audacity Croft decided to match this challenge by presenting that great question-mark play *Hamlet*.

The production received ecstatic notices; the *Daily Express* wrote: 'How pleasant to be able to commend a good cause, not because it is a cause but because it is good.' The *Daily Telegraph* went into considerable detail: 'The Youth Theatre's production of Shakespeare's *Hamlet* is notable for many things, most of all for the unequalled pleasure of hearing Shakespeare's poetry spoken with meaning, intelligence and beauty.

'Michael Croft's direction is incisive and straightforward with a masterly attention to detail which enabled the duel between Hamlet and Laertes to have its intended excitement and dignity to which the death of Hamlet was a fitting climax.

Hamlet,
*Scala Theatre,
1963. Simon Ward
as Hamlet.*

*he first Youth Theatre
roduction in 1956.
ichard Hampton* (Henry V)
the Crispin's Day scene.

'An uncluttered set with a minimum of distractions kept one's attention firmly on the players who were not dwarfed by the splendour of their costumes but wore them with a natural grace and ease of movement.'

The Times quite simply said: 'If it were necessary to offer any justification of the Youth Theatre's existence, this production is more than enough. One wonders how it is done and wishes it were done more often.'

60

Financially speaking, the saving factor came in the spring of 1960. Impressed by the critics' reception of *Hamlet*, Dutch managements pressed Croft to take the play to Holland where it was an incredible and instantaneous success with critics and public alike. Then, in May, the Youth Theatre went to Paris to take part in the international *Théâtre des Nations* Festival, as the official representatives of Britain.

Officialdom in Britain had been astounded at a young amateur company being given such an important invitation. One official body told Croft that they had no idea what on earth the Paris Festival was doing by inviting the Youth Theatre. When the company returned from Paris, however, officialdom was whistling a different tune, for again rave notices had met the performance.

One critic wrote: 'Our apprehensions were without foundation. The perilous venture proved a success, and such a success!' Another went even further: 'This *Hamlet*, performed by a young company who travelled specially from London, will be remembered as one of the great events of the present season at the *Théâtre des Nations*!'

In the 1960 summer season, again at the Queen's Theatre, the company pressed home its advantage by presenting, for the first time, its modern dress production of *Julius Caesar*. Ecstatic notices continued, as in the *Evening News*: 'The Youth Theatre is on the verge of becoming a permanent feature of the theatrical scene—and on the showing of its *Julius Caesar* last night this is thoroughly deserved.'

Bernard Levin wrote in the *Daily Express:* 'The sudden chill when the conspirators arrive at Brutus's house, of seeing that one of them is dressed as a police officer, another as a senior naval officer, is something I have not known in this play before; and the Teddy-boy murder of Cinna, the poet, is horribly modern and modernly horrible.

'It is enough to say that here is a production that can be wholeheartedly recommended, not because "they're very good for boys", but because they're very good!'

Even the hard-to-please *Punch* was abundant in its praise: 'Mr Croft is something of a genius with crowds, and he has made the herd stupidity of the Roman public really frightening . . .

'This production has such remarkable life and vigour, and the verse speaking is so good, that it is hard to remember that those of the cast who are not still at school have only just left.'

Critics of the standing of Harold Hobson and Irving Wardle compared it most favourably with professional productions.

Milton Schulman observed in the *Evening Standard* that '. . . there was a vigour and enthusiasm about this effort which would put to shame many a professional production.'

The production was revived six times in the next four years; it went on three foreign tours, on one of which it represented Britain at the

61

Julius Caesar, *BBC TV, 1964. Antony (Michael Cadman) stirs up the mob.*

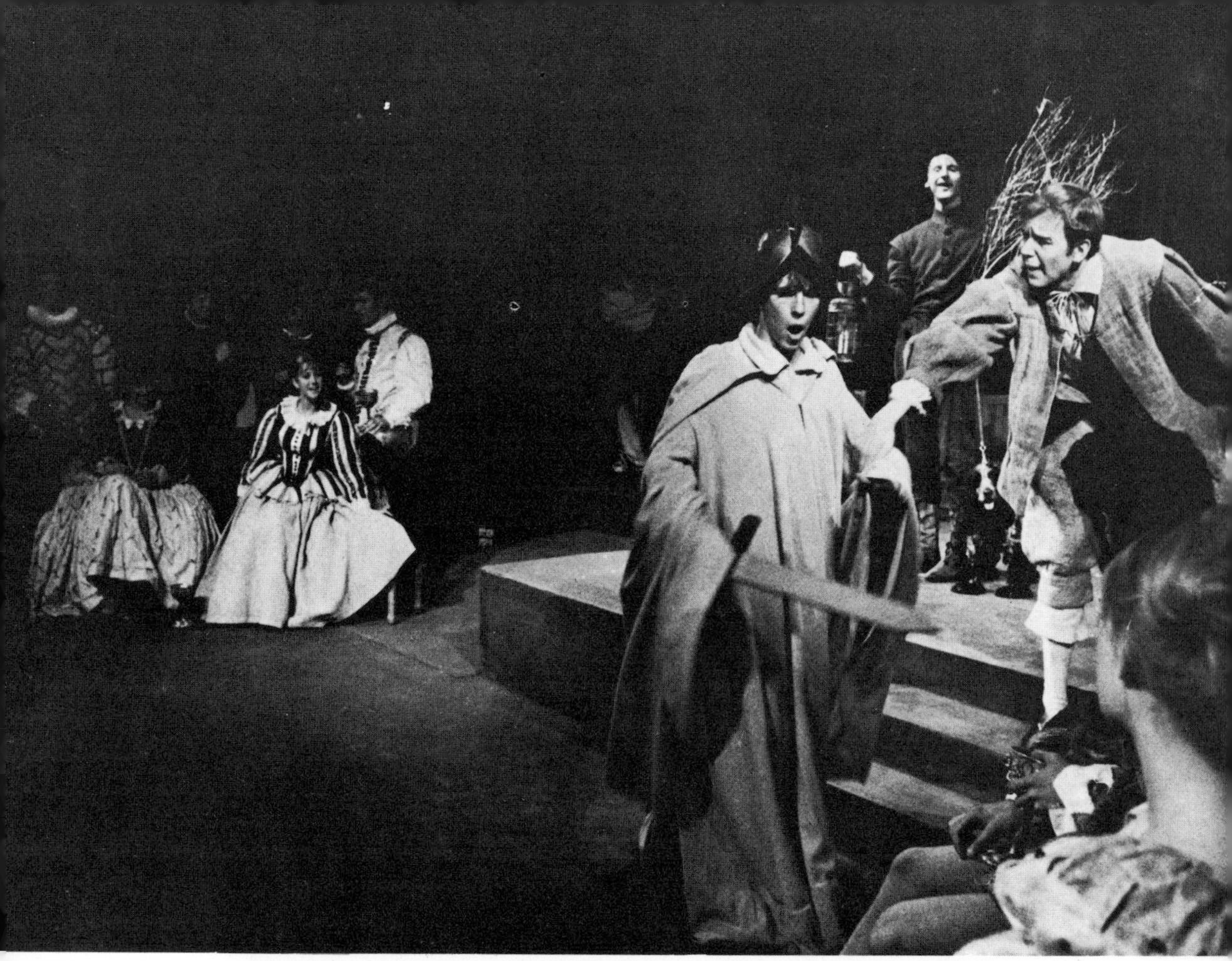

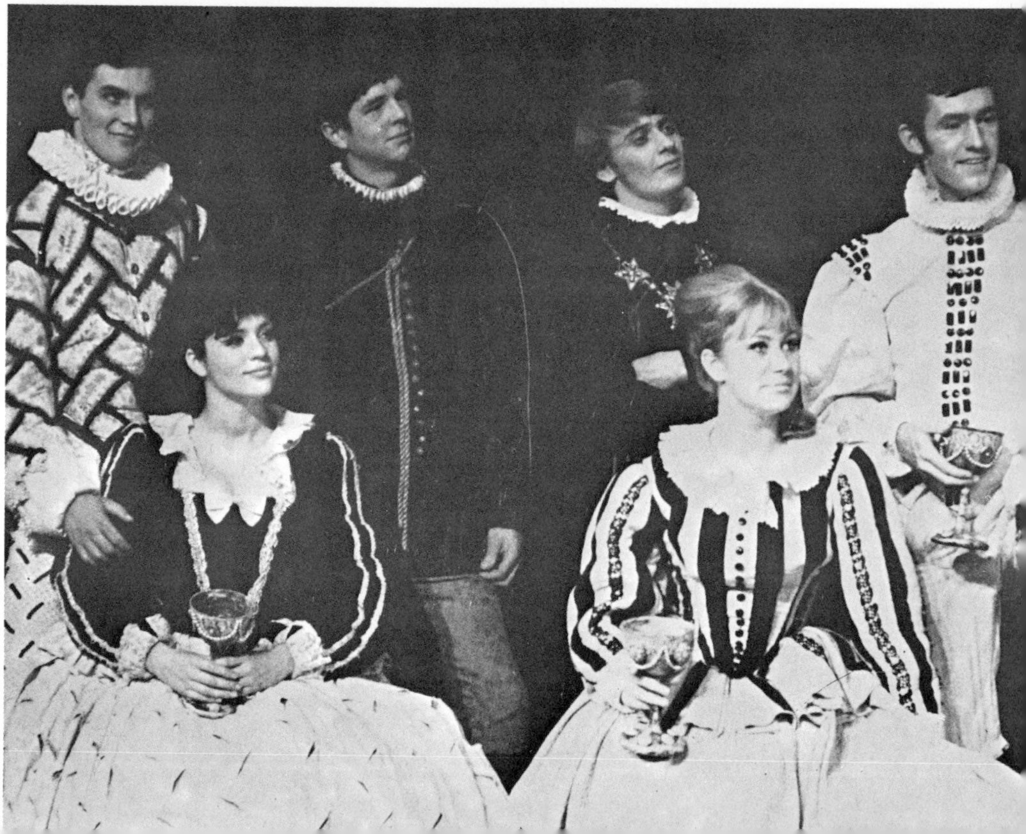

Berlin International Festival in 1961, and it became the first NYT production to be televised. In April 1964, as part of the quatercentenary celebrations of Shakespeare's birth, the newly inaugurated BBC 2 presented the entire production. The BBC have televised one of the NYT's productions each year since then.

In the eight years since that first production of *Julius Caesar* the NYT has more than consolidated its position and, judging by the critical receptions, it has maintained a consistently high standard. Bernard Levin observed that the company's 1964 production of *A Midsummer-Night's Dream* could 'stand the most favourable comparison with any professional staging of the play I have seen', and Herbert Kretzmer in the *Daily Express* said of *Coriolanus*, presented that same year: 'It deserves to outrun a dozen established West End successes. This production, indeed, is superior in every respect to the Mermaid's *Macbeth*, the Joan Littlewood *Henry IV* and even Sir Tyrone Guthrie's *Coriolanus* at Nottingham last year.'

63

For ten years it was the policy of the NYT to present only Shakespeare, but in the April of 1966 a small company presented Shaw's *The Devil's Disciple* in the Lake District. In the following summer season Croft continued and expanded this trend. Appearing for the first time at the Royal Court Theatre two companies presented Ben Jonson's *Bartholomew Fair* and David Halliwell's brilliant *Little Malcolm and His Struggle Against the Eunuchs*. With this latter play the company took one of its greatest risks by presenting an unestablished play. The risk, in fact, was two-fold, since *Little Malcolm*, when first presented professionally the previous February, had run for only two weeks despite excellent notices. By reviving the play so soon after its failure Croft was displaying two things—both his faith in a brilliant piece of dramatic writing, and also that the NYT had lost none of its courage or daring.

The play was ideally suited to the NYT since its five characters were young art students experiencing the problems, frustrations and tensions of all young people everywhere. So the risk was calculated; the gamble paid dividends.

The Times wrote: 'Mr Croft's direction is admirable; it seems unhurried, but moves at a splendid pace. The entire production does justice to an unusual but unlucky play,' while the *Daily Mail* trumpeted fanfares of acclaim: 'The NYT struck three blows in one last night; it gave its finest, most solidly professional production so far. Second, it tackled a contemporary play for the first time. Third,

it gave you a chance to see a new work by a new dramatist which anyone interested in the advance of art must see . . .

'Michael Croft, the director, gets remarkable performances out of his young cast. I honour his foolhardy courage, his faith, his uncanny skill and his success. He and his company have done the national adult theatre a service.'

Little Malcolm ran for a week at the Royal Court—the theatre was not available for longer. But during that week there were queues of people battling for tickets at the box office!

65

Now triumphantly launched into a completely new field of activity, the NYT took the next logical step by commissioning a new play specially from Peter Terson, who was, then, the resident playwright at the Victoria Theatre, Stoke-on-Trent. It was there Michael Croft saw one of his plays, *Jock-on-the-Go* and was so impressed by it that he immediately approached Terson about writing a play for the NYT. Terson agreed; the only condition he had to observe was that his play should cater for a very large cast.

By mid-spring of 1967 he had still not actually begun to write anything, but contacted Croft to say that he was thinking around the idea of a play based on football, with its supporters and hooliganism, but was worried that football might be square. Croft replied that football was anything but square, could not be more topical, and advised Terson that he should go ahead. So Terson started work on his play—which he called *Zigger-Zagger*.

There were many drafts of the play: I think almost everyone lost count of the number. Revisions and alterations, insertions, new scenes . . . we all knew that there was a play called *Zigger-Zagger* . . . or was it still all an amorphous mass of floating sheets of paper? I think it was only after the summer season had got under way and Terson had arrived in London that the play really began to take shape, and then it became a truly *ensemble* creation.

I have vivid memories of the few rehearsals I was able to watch—with two of the senior members of the cast pacing before the assembled chorus leading the chants, 'Zigger-zagger, Zigger-zagger, Oi, Oi, Oi!' 'We all live at the back of City End, the back of City End . . .' 'Ch, ch, ch, ch; ch, ch, ch, ch, yeh, yeh, yeh, yeh, oi, oi, oi!' Then bursting into song. In the corridor sat a pianist experimenting with tunes. He'd press-ganged everyone within reach into a choir that sang with rude gusto to tune after tune. Suggestions, ideas, experiments . . . something good! Do that again. Yes, keep it, must keep that in! And so on.

Bartholomew Fair, *Royal Court, 1966.*
Gwyneth Powell as Fat Urse.

Little Malcolm and his Struggle against the Eunuchs,
Royal Court, 1966. The Trial Scene. Wick (Tony May),
Malcolm (Tim Dalton), Ingham (Malcolm Storrey) and Nipple
(Barrie Rutter).

Michael Croft to Peter Terson: 'Peter, I think we could do with a couple more scenes in here . . .' The most remarkable sight of all: Peter Terson sitting cross-legged in the sun-drenched school yard, his typewriter before him, calmly knocking off two new scenes to order! This was instant creation, pure team work, exciting . . . fun!

Certainly Peter Terson provided the dialogue, but the cries, the chants, and explosions into ear-shattering song were the work of eighty dedicated, enthusiastic members.

Quite early during the rehearsals, because I had my typewriter with me in London, I was given the job of typing the script on to stencils for duplication. (The script I typed was as out of date, incomplete and inaccurate as the many others by the time the play went on. Only recently has a complete script of the play been compiled for publication by Penguin Books. At the time of performance many vital parts were carried simply in the actors' heads, having never appeared

Zigger-Zagger, *Jeannetta Cochrane Theatre, 1967.*
Harry (Nigel Humphries) is arrested for throwing a bottle at the police.

on paper!) To be honest I did not like the play over much when I typed it. I did not think that it had any special literary merit. But there lay my mistake. I was judging Terson's work on a literary and not a dramatic basis. I shall never forget the first time I saw the play on stage.

The Jeannetta Cochrane Theatre seats only four hundred and is intimate in a modern way. It seemed that the numbers on stage almost equalled the numbers in the audience. Suddenly the atmosphere became electric, and one was overwhelmed by a roof-raising blast of song which pinned one to the seat. A blaze of red and white, a blur of colour and movement, and a continuous swelling song. Such excitement, vitality and urgency! Pure theatre! This was a dramatic *experience* which neither I, nor anyone else who saw the play on stage, is likely to forget.

68

The Press went wild: 'A hit. Brilliantly conceived, totally original theatrical event.'—*Daily Express*. 'It's a sensation rare in London.'—*The Observer*. 'Fills one of the gaps in our literature. Vocally stupendous!'—*The Times*. 'Succeeded brilliantly.'—*Evening News*. 'Astonishing entertainment. Very funny. Blazes into the theatre like an immense animated crowd painting.'—*Sunday Times*. 'Brilliant. Fast and funny. I have not seen such an exciting and original first night of this kind since the great days of Joan Littlewood!'—*Daily Mail*.

Zigger-Zagger had a four-week run. From the end of the first week the bookings manager was having to turn people away from the doors, despite the addition of extra matinees. I was lucky enough to be able to see the play twice, and it thrilled me, excited me, moved me, overwhelmed me just as much the second time as the first.

Immediately the play went into production the cast spent all the time outside the performance at the BBC rehearsal studios preparing for a TV presentation, while an American impresario begged Michael Croft to let him take the play to Broadway. This, unfortunately, was impossible, since the cast had to return to school, college, or full-time jobs. But *Zigger-Zagger* was a spontaneous triumph of a kind the NYT had never known before. It has become a byword, and has done more than any other production in recent years to assert the NYT's vitality, and place it most resoundingly in the public and official eye. It was even voted by the London Theatre Critics in the 1967 *Plays and Players* poll, the most outstanding production to be seen in London during the year, and last September it was chosen to represent Britain at the Berlin International Festival.

6   National Youth Theatre members and membership

A reporter once described the NYT as: 'A Way of Life for those fortunate enough to be within its orbit.' He was entirely right, but when one tries to analyse why this is so one realises just how complex the NYT experience is.

One thing which the NYT is not is a Drama School; nor is it intended to fulfil a Drama School's main functions. It is simply an *ensemble* experience in practical theatre. Michael Croft's constant fear over the years has been that people will apply to join the company thinking it is an easy short-cut to stardom. It is not. It is inevitable, however, that some members should become professional actors, and in these cases Croft and his staff will give all the help they can, providing the member has been a good Youth Theatre member, and worked well for the company. As with all other societies one must not expect to take out more than one puts in. It is interesting to note that of this very small percentage of the NYT's total membership who go on to become professionals (only about ten per cent) most usually fare well in this most competitive world, and that names like Simon Ward, Michael York, Martin Jarvis, Neil Stacey, Jane Merrow, Richard Hampton, Kenneth Farrington, Hywel Bennett, Ian McShane, Antony May, Ken Cranham, Tim Dalton and Helen Mirren first appeared in NYT programmes.

When I asked some of my friends who have become professionals what the NYT meant to them they nearly all answered in professional terms—that is, how it helped them with their training and career. Ken Cranham reminded me that the later part of their NYT experience coincided exactly with their Drama School training, and thus it was difficult to separate the two, or look objectively at their time with the NYT. However, on one point they all agreed: the NYT provided a most necessary and refreshing change to Drama School. One RADA student described returning to the NYT as 'coming up to the surface for fresh air'. Martin Jarvis explains this further:

'At RADA, inevitably, one was concerned with all the technical accoutrements of becoming an actor: starting to learn how to move, improving one's vocal range, learning how to time laughs—in fact working on all the external means of conveying a character to an audience. Not surprisingly one's performance at RADA at this time suffered from a surfeit of 'technique', and a certain lack of inner truth. So the Youth Theatre plays that one did during the vacation had a tremendous value for those of us who were working to become professionals.

70

'Croft's way of working was almost to let you find out for yourself what you wanted to do in a part—the framework of the scene took shape alongside your performance. You were never strait-jacketed into making a move because a move was needed to complete a visual pattern—action always emerged from the natural thought and decisions of the character.'

Both Helen Mirren and Michael York emphasised the value of the company discipline—not an imposed discipline, but one which is self-taught by necessity, and both lauded the cosmopolitanism of the company.

Richard III, *Scala Theatre, 1963. Richard (Neil Stacey), Catesby (Robert East), Ratcliffe (Kenneth Cranham), Lovell (Clive Emsley).*

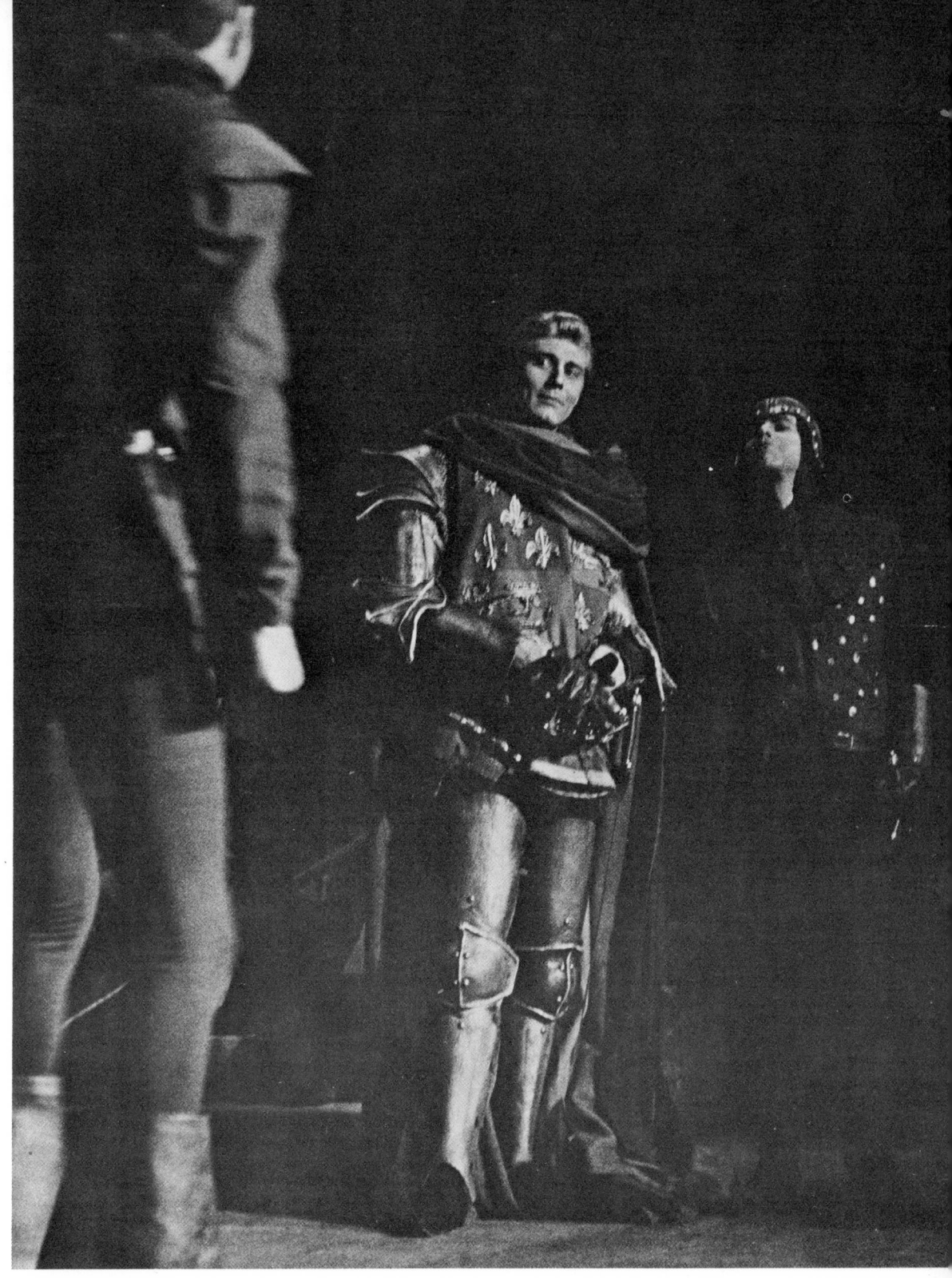

The Glove Scene, Henry V *at Sadlers Wells, 1962.*
Williams (Michael Cadman), Henry V (Martin Jarvis) and Fluellen (Geoffrey Hutching).

F

Troilus (Andrew Murray) and Diomedes (Tim Dalton) in
Troilus and Cressida, *Old Vic, 1965.*

Helen Mirren says: 'Coming as I did from a smallish provincial town and convent school, it opened a far wider social life than I could otherwise have expected, perhaps at first too wide. Being plunged into the middle of so many new faces made me very shy and inhibited at first. It was in the NYT, however, that I made many of my greatest friends, and even now, two years after my last season, there are a mass of people centred around the NYT headquarters, some new, some old, that I have an immediate interest in and communication with.' Michael York endorses this: 'The company is drawn from all walks of life, so that any narrowing of background caused by class or education was immediately remedied by the Youth Theatre's lively catholicism.'

Jane Merrow was probably the most objective of all, looking at the NYT in terms of the overall theatrical scene of which, despite its amateur status, it is very much a part: 'Because this is a company of young people, not all of whom may have outstanding talent, the NYT cannot afford to play tricks on the public, or seek the slick sensationalism which has contaminated the professional theatre. Amidst the sickness of 'pop' theatre and the 'theatre of the absurd', while directors ever more frequently turn to gimmicks, the NYT remains one true bastion of meaningful, honest theatre. Michael Croft seeks for the play's true meaning, allowing the texts to do their job unimpeded.

'What is more, just at this time when entertainment in its worst sense is spoon-fed to people, the NYT offers young folk the chance to actively participate and to direct their energies and thoughts outwards rather than in—which denies unhealthy introversion . . . Oh, and I must add that I was so happy with the NYT—I wouldn't have missed it for the world!'

So a more rounded picture of the NYT experience begins to emerge through the testament of past members. But there is still so much more . . . To get at the heart of the experience I asked friends still with the company what it all meant to them. Time and time again the answer came back—'I can't say. It's too intangible to put my finger on.' Even so, they made valiant attempts at my impossible question.

Tim Haunton, now the 'old man' of the company, having been a member for eight years, said: 'First, the Youth Theatre introduced me to some of my dearest friends. This is of primary significance for me. It made me read all of Shakespeare: it's second great merit. Youth Theatre taught me that almost anything is possible if people co-operate with each other. The enthusiasm and sheer physical energy which I have seen at work on productions always brings results. The summer seasons are always born into confusion; perhaps we haven't a theatre or a set or enough money. Constant improvisation from the actor, technician or director is a first demand. Things will always be going wrong but results are required. So the Youth Theatre encourages a bold assessment of situations in order to reach direct solutions. Be brave: the valuable advice it offers; laugh too, and you'll survive a rigorous but most rewarding experience.'

His remark about friends was echoed in nearly all the replies I received, and is one of the most important facets of the NYT for me. I agree with Nigel Humphries that it is amazing that such strong friendships can be created when 'you only meet these people for two months of the year, and then perhaps once or twice more during the year'. Nigel went on to say: 'Although people may find that they have

Falstaff (David Weston) in the Tavern Scene
with Pistol (Ian McShane) and Drawer
(Tim Haunton).

The Traitor Scen
Scroop (Giles Block), Westmoreland (John Shrapnel
Hastings (Bill Perce), Lancaster (Paul Hil
and Mowbray (Jeremy Rowe

Henry IV Part 2,
Apollo Theatre, 1961.

a great deal to do and long hours to work, it is the spirit it is done in which makes it all worth while.' This was echoed again by Chris Smith, the NYT's Stage Director.

Chris wrote: 'It may sound pretentious, but the NYT helped me to grow up, both by meeting people outside my particular social sphere, and by the imposition of a demanding self discipline. The marvellous thing about the NYT is that the convivial atmosphere is maintained year after year, and that whatever your position is in the organisation you know that the whole company is working towards one aim. To say that the main objective of the NYT—that of staging productions— is the all-important thing is wrong. What is important is all that the staging of these productions entails.'

75

When I asked people, 'Why do you keep on coming back, year after year?' I found that people could only say, 'There's something which makes us, something we can't define.' The Youth Theatre magic? The coming together of so many sides and aspects of life, so many different experiences rolled into one? Perhaps one reply which comes near to being a complete answer comes from Jon Perzucek.

'I never knew what the Youth Theatre was about until I came to London for the 1966 production of *Antony and Cleopatra*. This was not my first night away from home for I used to be an enthusiastic voyager of England. However, it was the first time I had ever been to London. Arriving late one Tuesday evening I had nowhere to stay and consequently popped round to Eccleston with a friend who introduced me to Michael Croft once more. I spent the night wrapped in army blankets at the club headquarters, surrounded by photographs of past plays which intrigued me immensely. How could people appear so fervent and yet so poised?

'I groped my way that season, and yet one thing became apparent— that in the Youth Theatre you are never wrapped up in a plastic bag but become part of the product whether actor or technician. Even if you are given a ten-foot banner to parade or a non-rubber hammer to wield, and even if you live on bird-seed you are never allowed to fly away from an unaccomplished task. Maybe it is strictly a matter of conscience but for the most part you feel responsible for your actions to the group as a whole.

'You will be working hard, catching tubes, flogging leaflets to Americans, rehearsing up and down and down and up, or lugging scenery from place to place. The Youth Theatre is no joy ride, but I came back. It had gripped me, made me aware of new things, people and personalities.

'Above all it is the people which attract me back year after year. None of them are either what could be called 'arty' or 'basic', yet all have qualities which make them individuals in a crowd. To meet them all is like a cascade of flower-power happiness!'

But still I believe there is more over and above these remarks by my friends. Is it simply in order to live in London for two months, to take part in a production and see their friends that members often make big sacrifices? That they take any spare-time job that's going, rehearse all day and perhaps work half the night, just to earn some money on which to live? Ron Smerzcak spent a good part of the *Romeo and Juliet* season getting up at seven in the morning, walking to the Enterprise to swab down the bars and clean the tables, all for a few shillings and breakfast each day. Some members turn their hands to charring, or serving in cafés, washing taxis, serving behind bars . . . There are actually *two* common, binding factors between members: that all are working towards one end, and that nearly all are financially very poor for a very large part of the time. The community spirit is indescribable. What evenings at the Enterprise! What parties! In flats ranging across London from Camden to Kensington. What late-night sessions of records, jokes and laughter. One looks forward to the penniless friend who comes to make use of one's floor for the night, to the penny-stakes brag sessions, to the whole spectrum of activity which comprises an NYT season. When life in general is such a complicated process, life with the NYT seems so much simpler and happier. It is communal existence, and that well-worn saying, 'All for one and one for all', could not find a happier, more truthful expression anywhere else than with the NYT. And that, I think, is the thing which has made me long to get back with the company, year after year. Maybe it's unorthodox, but it is only what each member makes of it, for each member has to make his or her own decisions. It is an exercise in accepting responsibility, in learning how to live, while enjoying at the same time a quite unforgettable experience.

7 The future (a home of our own)

Although the NYT has received an annual grant from the Department of Education and Science since 1960, this covers less than half the round-the-year running costs, so that its existence has been a catalogue of struggles for survival. In the early days it came very near to disaster through lack of finances on several occasions. It still walks a tightrope between security and the abyss of financial ruin. But it was in 1957, 1958 and 1961 particularly that the Youth Theatre wobbled precariously on the brink of total disaster.

After the calamitous appearance in Manchester in August 1957, the Youth Theatre looked as though it could not possibly continue. Despite the company's valiant endeavours to secure audiences during that week in Manchester, lodging in most extraordinary accommoda-

Richard II, Apollo Theatre, 1961. The Dying Gaunt (Colin Farrell). Background: York (Neil Stacey), Northumberland (Paul Hill), Ross and Willoughby (Michael Cadman and Robin Ellis).

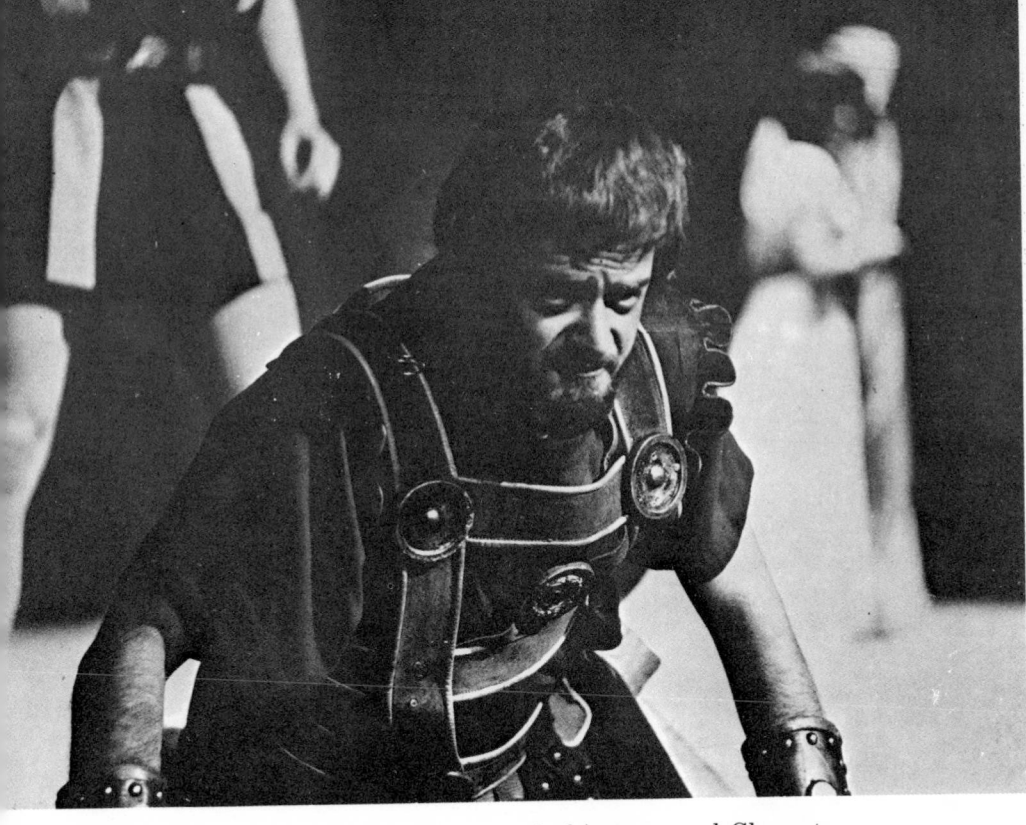

Clive Emlsey as Antony in the revival of Antony and Cleopatra
at the Scala Theatre, 1966.

tion including the mission of an obscure religious sect, they left
Manchester exhausted and very heavily in the red.

Croft spent six months endeavouring to raise funds by contacting
industrialists, patrons of the arts and charitable organisations, but
at the end of this time he had nothing to show for his efforts. In
1958, however, the Youth Theatre received a £500 grant from the
King George's Jubilee Trust, while at the same time Len Ward,
Simon Ward's father, was busy collecting almost £400 from his
colleagues in the motor trade; for the moment the Youth Theatre
could again look forward with some confidence.

It was unfortunate, therefore, that they had a crack at the Edin-
burgh Festival, for that year there were twenty-six productions
competing for audiences at the Festival and though the Youth
Theatre's *Troilus and Cressida* received excellent Press notices, plus
the approval of Professor Dover Wilson, the company found itself

playing to virtually empty houses. Again the Youth Theatre was heavily in the red.

It was in 1959, when things seemed blackest, that hope appeared in the form of Dorothy Elmhirst, a staunch patron of the Arts, who invited the Youth Theatre to Dartington Hall in Devon, and, following its success there with *Hamlet*, engineered its transfer to the Queen's Theatre in London for the NYT's first ever West End season. Although the company made a small profit at the Queen's, this was almost all lost when the play transferred again to the Lyric, Hammersmith, so the company was still by no means out of deep water.

Suddenly two more friends of the Youth Theatre appeared—Miss Vivian and Miss Olga Veevers, enthusiastic supporters of both the theatre and cricket, who had supported the Youth Theatre in the form of small donations for a number of years. Now, they declared, the Youth Theatre had proved its point, and they were ready to support it to the tune of £500 per year.

Since 1962 the NYT has been assisted by the *Daily Mail* with a contribution towards production costs each year. It owes a great deal to the enthusiasm of Mike Randall, the late editor, and his successor Arthur Brittenden, and especially to the efforts of Roy Nash their Education Correspondent.

Without the help of these generous people, and all the other friends who regularly send donations amounting in total to something like £200 a year, one wonders if the Youth Theatre would have survived at all. They, as much as anyone, made it possible for the Youth Theatre to expand and move forward, to such an extent that by 1964 it had become obvious to Michael Croft that, for the NYT to continue growing, it desperately needed a home of its own. Each year the company ran into difficulties regarding advance publicity and booking, since it was not sure which theatre it would be occupying until well into the season. Also, on a simple, practical level, it seemed that it would be impossible to continue recruiting on the present scale without facilities to stage more plays.

Thus, in 1964, plans for the NYT Centre were announced. It was envisaged that the Centre would incorporate a wide range of activities, have its own theatre, rehearsal rooms, workshop, dance hall, games rooms, recording studios, quiet rooms, library, restaurant, arts and crafts studios, plus club rooms and living quarters for the Youth Theatre companies appearing at the Centre. It was proposed that not only would the Centre be the home of the NYT for its summer season,

Coriolanus, *Queens Theatre, 1964*
Tullus Aufidius (Robert East
triumphs over Coriolanus
(John Nightingale)

Antony (John Nightingale), Lepidus (Frank Sowerby), and Caesar (Tim Meats) in Antony and Cleopatra, *Old Vic, 1965.*

but also be available for the use of any other Youth Theatre company. Lastly, Croft intended to inaugurate a professional NYT company which would be based at the Centre for half the year, playing especially to young audiences and touring the country for the other six months.

The Centre would be a fixed, focal point entirely aimed at catering for young people. It would be available for all young people living close to it for use throughout the year, and be a place where they might find whatever activity they desired, be it jazz, pop, judo— anything! Taking into account that large school parties already attend NYT productions from as far away as Nottingham, Southampton, Ipswich, Birmingham and Leicester, it would be quite logical to suppose that more and more schools would attend the Centre once it was established. Indeed, an enormous number of schools have pledged support in the form of sending parties, and have said that such a Centre is not so much an optional luxury as a necessity!

A very special emphasis would be placed on plays which were being studied in the schools. Also, however, new plays by new playwrights would be presented; the Centre would have the facilities to experiment and thereby play a very important part in the overall theatrical scene, being a show-case for new writers. The scheme was a logical progression for the NYT, and a very necessary one. It would make it possible for the annual intake into the NYT to be vastly increased, and the Centre would become one of the most vital and prominent amenities in the entire Youth Service field.

The scheme received immediate, enthusiastic support from the Press, Parliament, the professional theatre and educational circles, but enthusiasm was not enough. The Centre was likely to cost £300,000, and although the NYT campaigned with all its old vigour and succeeded in obtaining a magnificent site in the Borough of Camden, it could not obtain the vital support it needed from official bodies, such as The Arts Council; and now, four years after the scheme was first announced, the architect's plans are going yellow and stale on the NYT's walls.

However, at the very time of writing, a ray of hope has appeared. Camden Council have generously offered the NYT, not the long-cherished Centre, but a small theatre now being built in Euston Road,

Richard III, Scala Theatre, 1960. A Youth Theatre charge.

next to St Pancras Station. It will be called The Shaw Theatre, and it should be ready by early 1970. The NYT will then be able to form even more young amateur companies, and will form its first professional young company to play there for several months of the year.

Since all the above was written, the NYT has had more triumphs at home and abroad. It has had another fantastic success in London with a new Peter Terson play, *The Apprentices,* and both this and *Zigger-Zagger* have been presented as major productions on BBC Television.

At the 1968 Holland Festival, the NYT was acclaimed for its production of *Little Malcolm,* and later in the year, at the Berlin International Festival, its production of *Zigger-Zagger* was unanimously hailed in the German Press as the 'hit' of the Festival. 'There is an explosion in the theatre,' said *Die Welt,* 'that will be remembered for a long time and that restores one's faith in the theatre.'

In fact, 1968 may prove to have been the NYT's most important year to date. It not only staged six productions with outstanding success, but it at last won its long battle for all-important recognition from the Arts Council. The Council had always refused to support the NYT on the grounds that it could not assist amateur companies, and it is a great pleasure to me to be able to report, almost as a postscript, that the Arts Council has now decided that the NYT can no longer be ignored and has offered it a grant of £5,000 a year.

The Apprentices, *Jeannetta Cochrane Theatre, 1968.*
Linda (Paula Wilcox) and Betty (Kathleen Lee)
watch Bagley (Barrie Rutter) and Harry (Tony Phipps)
dancing to 'Parade of the Pops'.

Glossary

Stage Manager	The person who liases between the Director and actors during rehearsal, and during performance is responsible for the running of the show.
ASM	Assistant Stage Manager, often prompter and looks after props.
Pan	The sound effects equipment.
Blocking	The giving of the first, basic moves at the beginning of rehearsals.
Get-in	The moving into the theatre of the set and props.
Fit-up	The erection in the theatre of the set.
Technical Run	The first time the actors run the play in costume and make-up with music and lights in the theatre, the intention being to ensure that the whole production 'works' . . . that the lighting and music are right etc.